DATE DUE

GAYLORD			PRINTED IN U.S.A.

Famous Biographies for Young People

FAMOUS AMERICAN POETS

FAMOUS VIOLINISTS FOR YOUNG PEOPLE

FAMOUS PIANISTS FOR YOUNG PEOPLE

FAMOUS COMPOSERS FOR YOUNG PEOPLE

MODERN COMPOSERS FOR YOUNG PEOPLE

FAMOUS MEN OF MEDICINE

FAMOUS AUTHORS FOR YOUNG PEOPLE

FAMOUS EXPLORERS FOR YOUNG PEOPLE

FAMOUS GENERALS AND ADMIRALS FOR YOUNG PEOPLE

FAMOUS KINGS AND QUEENS FOR YOUNG PEOPLE

FAMOUS PIONEERS FOR YOUNG PEOPLE

FAMOUS BRITISH NOVELISTS

FAMOUS BRITISH POETS

FAMOUS MODERN AMERICAN NOVELISTS

FAMOUS INVENTORS FOR YOUNG PEOPLE

FAMOUS AMERICAN NEGROES

FAMOUS OLD MASTERS OF PAINTING

FAMOUS NATURALISTS

FAMOUS AMERICAN STATESMEN

FAMOUS HUMANITARIANS

FAMOUS SCIENTISTS

FAMOUS WOMEN OF AMERICA

FAMOUS WOMEN SINGERS

FAMOUS ENGINEERS

FAMOUS SIGNERS OF THE DECLARATION

FAMOUS NEGRO MUSIC MAKERS

FAMOUS AMERICAN PAINTERS

FAMOUS DANCERS

FAMOUS AMERICAN MEN OF LETTERS

FAMOUS NEGRO HEROES OF AMERICA

FAMOUS AMERICAN HUMORISTS

FAMOUS MODERN AMERICAN WOMEN WRITERS

FAMOUS FRENCH PAINTERS

FAMOUS LATIN-AMERICAN LIBERATORS

FAMOUS AMERICAN ACTORS AND ACTRESSES

FAMOUS INDUSTRIALISTS

FAMOUS AMERICAN PIONEERING WOMEN

FAMOUS MODERN NEWSPAPER WRITERS

FAMOUS UNDERWATER ADVENTURERS

FAMOUS AMERICAN SPIES

FAMOUS AMERICAN MILITARY LEADERS OF WORLD WAR II

FAMOUS AMERICAN ATHLETES

FAMOUS PIONEERS IN SPACE

FAMOUS MODERN EXPLORERS

FAMOUS PRESIDENTS OF THE UNITED STATES

FAMOUS MAKERS OF AMERICA

FAMOUS LAWMEN OF THE OLD WEST

FAMOUS AMERICAN WOMEN ATHLETES

FAMOUS FIGHTERS OF WORLD WAR I

FAMOUS POETS FOR YOUNG PEOPLE

FAMOUS TWENTIETH CENTURY LEADERS

FAMOUS NEGRO ATHLETES

FAMOUS AMERICAN NEGRO POETS

FAMOUS INSTRUMENTALISTS

FAMOUS MERCHANTS

FAMOUS
INSTRUMENTALISTS

FAMOUS INSTRUMENTALISTS

by David Ewen

ILLUSTRATED WITH PHOTOGRAPHS

FAMOUS BIOGRAPHIES
DM
FOR YOUNG PEOPLE

Dodd, Mead & Company · New York

Bq

Printed in the United States of America
by Vail-Ballou Press, Inc., Binghamton, N. Y.

INTRODUCTORY NOTE

A living art renews itself generation after generation—even grows stronger. This is particularly true of the interpretative art in music. Our greatest instrumentalists have fed on the traditions, experiences, and achievements of the great musicians who had preceded them; then they went on to create traditions, experiences, and achievements of their own. The result is that performance in every area of music is on a much higher technical and artistic level today than it was a century ago. If we need any proof on this score we have only to remember how, years ago, even world-famous instrumentalists first coming into contact with works like Tchaikovsky's *Violin Concerto*, Brahms's *Violin Concerto* and *Second Piano Concerto*, and Paganini's *Caprices*, and so forth, often regarded these works as unplayable—so exacting and advanced did the technical demands of this music appear in those days. Today these works are negotiated with facility even by conservatory students.

This volume is an attempt to introduce to young music lovers the generation of great virtuosos who have come to the fore around the world since the end of World War II. Many are already established as concert fixtures, others are well on their way to becoming so. Biographical information is combined with critical and personal material. From time to time a historical perspective is also introduced.

To present the concert life in all its variety this book has included not only violinists, pianists, and cellists, but also two two-piano teams, and one performer on the guitar and lute. Many of these artists are being discussed within a book for the first time. All represent the vanguard of a new generation of performing greats in music.

CONTENTS

Illustrations follow page 64

INTRODUCTORY NOTE 7

VAN CLIBURN (1934–) 13

LEON FLEISHER (1928–) 29

GARY GRAFFMAN (1918–)—BYRON
JANIS (1928–) 37

GLENN GOULD (1932–) 49

ISAAC STERN (1920–) 57

LEONARD ROSE (1918–) 69

EUGENE ISTOMIN (1925–) 75

RUGGIERO RICCI (1920–)—JAIME
LAREDO (1941–) 81

PIERRE FOURNIER (1906–) 91

EMIL GILELS (1916–) 97

SVIATOSLAV RICHTER (1914–) 103

DAVID OISTRAKH (1908–) 111

MSTISLAV ROSTROPOVICH (1927–) 119

9

CONTENTS

DANIEL BARENBOIM (1942–   )   125

SHMUEL ASHKENASI (1941–   )—DAVID
  BAR-ILIAN (1930–   )   131

WHITTEMORE (1916–   ) AND LOWE
  (1917–   )—GOLD (1919–   ) AND
  FIZDALE (1920–   )   137

JULIAN BREAM (1933–   )   147

INDEX   153

FAMOUS
INSTRUMENTALISTS

VAN CLIBURN

[1934–   ]

𝒟URING THE 1957–1958 concert season Van Cliburn was booked for his fourth American tour in which he made twenty appearances. He was receiving on the average of $1,000 for each of these concerts. After the necessary deductions were made—travel expenses, managers' fees, and so forth—he netted for the entire year less than $10,000. All this represented a comedown from the two previous seasons. In 1955–1956 he had been booked for thirty concerts, and in 1956–1957 for twenty-three concerts. A consistent and perceptible decline in both his popularity and fortune could hardly escape the notice of either Van Cliburn himself or his manager.

But less than a year after that fourth tour a miracle took place. For 1958–1959 Cliburn was getting more engagements than he could possibly handle, all over the map. He was now receiving between $2,500 and $4,000 for each concert. The Steve Allen "Tonight" show on television stood ready to pay him $3,000 to play a few numbers. (The last time that Cliburn had appeared on the Steve Allen show, in 1955, his fee was only $75.00!) He also made his first recording, which forthwith became the first classical long-playing disk to sell more than a million copies.

These figures, amazing though they are, tell only part of the story of what had happened to Van Cliburn. In 1958 he was the first musican ever to get a New York ticker-tape parade. He received at that time the Medallion of the City of New York and the Scroll of the City "for exceptional and distinguished services." A festive dinner was given in his honor at the Waldorf-Astoria Hotel where the political, social, and musical elite of New York City paid him extravagant tributes. His concert at Carnegie Hall on May 19, 1958, drew the largest advance box-office sale in the history of that historic auditorium, with speculators charging as much as $100 for a pair of tickets. The younger generation mobbed him wherever he went.

What had caused this miracle? What had transformed a comparatively unknown concert artist into one of the greatest box-office draws and one of the most adulated musicians on the American musical scene—and within the period of less than a year?

The answer is—a musical competition.

Winning first prize in a musical competition, even an international one, did not always bring about such happy results. There have been many instances in which young American artists captured the highest honors in some of the most highly esteemed competitions without any effect at the box office. With Van Cliburn, however, it had been a case of being at the right place and at the right time. And that made all the difference.

The place was Moscow. The time was during the first slight thaw in the frozen relations between the United States and the Soviet Union. For a decade the Iron Curtain had separated the

14

two powers. Any exchange of ideas, personalities, or cultural relationships had been either difficult or altogether impossible. Then, in the summer of 1955, during a summit meeting in Geneva, Switzerland, a decision was reached between President Eisenhower and Premier Khrushchev for a fluid cultural exchange between the United States and the Soviet Union. It was this agreement that made it possible for Van Cliburn to enter the Tchaikovsky Competition, an international contest for pianists inaugurated in Moscow in 1958.

Those who were responsible for getting Van Cliburn to enter the competition—and who raised the funds needed to get him to Moscow and back—were not sanguine about his chances of winning the first prize. Not that they doubted his musical or pianistic gifts, which they regarded as truly phenomenal! What they did doubt seriously, however, was whether the Soviet Union would permit an American to walk off with the laurels however much he deserved them. In light of the cold war, it seemed unthinkable for the political and musical powers of the Soviet Union—childishly jealous of their own accomplishments in all fields of endeavor—to allow the world to know that an American had bested the Soviets in one of their own competitions.

In spite of such doubts Cliburn's friends and sponsors felt that the gamble of his going to the Soviet Union was worth taking. The reason for their decision was the rather unpalatable fact that Van Cliburn's appeal to American audiences as a concert performer was rapidly beginning to dwindle. There was no question of his musical attainments. Already he was considered one of the most brilliant and uniquely endowed young pianists to emerge in many a year. But, as so often happens in America's concert life, public interest in a young native son has a brief span. In lavishing its adulation on the world figures in music, most Americans tend to slight those who have yet to reach the upper stratosphere of recognition and fame.

What Cliburn needed at this critical juncture in his career was the limelight of world attention pinned strongly and squarely on both his personality and his talent. Such a limelight could come from Moscow, if, miraculously, he did manage to capture the first prize. Such an award would be news of international importance and scope and would, by the same token, generate a new interest in his remarkable gifts. This is the way Cliburn's sponsors, teacher, and friends argued. And this is why they were determined to send him to Moscow.

Van Cliburn, aged twenty-three, had by no means been a musician without honor or recognition before winning the Moscow prize that made him such an international celebrity. Since his prodigy days he had gathered one prize and honor after another with the giant scoop of his huge arms: the Texas Prize in 1947; the G. B. Dealey Memorial Award in Dallas, Texas, in 1954; the Chopin Scholarship in 1952; the Carl M. Roeder Memorial Award in 1954; and, most important of all, the Leventritt Award (the oldest and most significant contest for instrumentalists in the United States) in 1954. A Van Cliburn day was celebrated in his home town of Kilgore, Texas, in 1954.

Discriminating musicians, the musical elite, the cognoscenti were fully aware of his capabilities. When Abram Chasins (himself a concert pianist in his younger years, though now the musical director of radio station WQXR in New York) heard him play the music of Bach, Mozart, Beethoven, and Chopin during the Chopin Scholarship Competition, he

16

insisted that he had never "seen equaled in a competition [such] a demonstration of pianism, sensitivity, and showmanship." George Szell and Dimitri Mitropoulos, each a world-famous symphony conductor, and each serving as one of the judges of the Leventritt Award, were no less enthusiastic. "He is remarkable," commented Szell. Mitropoulos exclaimed: "He is fantastic. His playing is wizardry."

The Leventritt Award entitled its winner to appear as soloist with several major orchestras, including the New York Philharmonic. When Cliburn made the first of these appearances—he played Tchaikovsky's *First Piano Concerto* with the New York Philharmonic on November 15, 1954, Mitropoulos conducting—he was given a rousing ovation by the audience. In the New York *World Telegram* Louis Biancolli reported: "This is one of the most genuine and refreshing keyboard talents to come out of the West—or anywhere else—in a long time. Van Cliburn is obviously going places, except that he plays like he had already been there."

In 1954 his concert career began in earnest, under the management of Judson, O'Neill, and Judd. First he made a brilliant appearance on commercial TV, on the Steve Allen "Tonight" show, on January 19, 1955. The switchboard became clogged with enthusiastic telephone messages. After that came his first tour of the United States, each stop an outstanding success.

But with his second and third tours Van Cliburn's career began to wilt. He had ceased to be a novelty. But for winning the much-publicized Tchaikovsky Award in Moscow in 1958, Van Cliburn would, in all probability, have suffered the same kind of comparative neglect experienced by so many other of the younger American virtuosos who must compete in the music market with giants such as Artur Rubinstein, Rudolf

17

Serkin, Nathan Milstein, or Jascha Heifetz. The Moscow competition, however, proved the "shot in the arm" Cliburn's career needed so badly. Overnight he was lifted by the first prize in that contest to the Alpine peaks of success.

Van Cliburn had given proof of his remarkable musical gifts early. He was born in Shreveport, Louisiana, on July 12, 1934. The name on the birth certificate reads "Harvey Lavan Cliburn, Jr.," but from babyhood on he was never called anything but "Van." He was only three when he started picking out on the piano tunes he had heard his mother's pupils play—his mother being a piano teacher. This convinced the mother to give him lessons. At four he was already sufficiently advanced to appear in public. By five, when he was enrolled in public school, he was completely at home with musical symbols although he had not yet learned to read or write English.

By the time the family moved to Kilgore, Texas—where the father found a job with a petroleum factory—Van and his piano were inseparable. The father was by no means in favor of having his son practicing all the time—particularly when, coming home from work one evening, he saw how pale and drawn the child was after having spent several hours at the keyboard. The father tried to lure the boy to outdoor play by buying him roller skates, a bicycle, and a football. But Van gave no more than a passing glance at these and similar gifts. He stuck to the piano. Once, when the father was particularly persistent in trying to get Van to go outdoors and play with friends, and give less time to the piano, the child cried out: "Please, Father, don't say such things! I'm going to be a concert pianist."

During the summer of 1947 Van (aged thirteen) came to

New York with his mother. For a few months he attended the Juilliard School of Music for the study of musical theory, dictation, and sight reading. In every area he proved a most extraordinary pupil. That same year he competed as pianist for the Texas State Prize. In a twenty-one-day period he committed to memory the Tchaikovsky *First Piano Concerto*, played it in Houston, and won both first prize and a standing ovation. Later the same year, as Texas winner in the National Music Festival contest, he was brought to New York to repeat his performance of the Tchaikovsky *Concerto* in Carnegie Hall; once again all those who heard him were overwhelmed.

He continued concertizing, mainly in Texas; and he continued studying the piano with his mother until 1951 when she began to recognize that he needed more advanced training. They now returned to New York with the aim of entering Van as a pupil of Rosina Lhevinne at the Juilliard School of Music. After he had registered, Van discovered, to his intense disappointment, that her class was full, that he would have to be assigned to one of her assistants. He sought out Mme. Lhevinne and insisted on playing for her. She caught her breath as he went through Liszt's *Twelfth Hungarian Rhapsody*, and then and there accepted him as a private pupil. After studying with her for a year Cliburn won a grant from the Olga Samaroff Foundation, and the first prize in a concerto contest for pianists at the Juilliard School. Upon graduating from Juilliard in 1954 he received the Roeder Award for "outstanding achievement in piano." Later the same year he not only captured the much-coveted Leventritt Award but had also been signed by Arthur Judson for his first concert tour. Before offering Cliburn the contract, Judson had consulted Mme. Lhevinne and William Schuman, the latter then president of

Juilliard. They told him in no uncertain terms that they regarded Van Cliburn "tops" among the younger pianists.

That first tour, as we have remarked, was successful, and so was his first appearance on television. His second television appearance, a year later, and his next two tours were comparative "duds." It was at this crucial point in Van Cliburn's career that he went to Moscow.

The announcement of a contest for pianists in Moscow reached Mme. Lhevinne early in 1958. She put it aside without giving it a second thought at the time; she had serious doubts whether any American musician would get a fair hearing in a Soviet competition. Later that day, looking out of the window, she suddenly said to herself: "If *anybody* can win it, Van can." From that moment on she became a dynamo. First she had to convince Van to go, then she had to raise the money needed for his trip.

Van spent three months of intensive piano practice in getting ready for the contest. At times he worked as many as ten hours a day, seven days a week.

Forty-eight young artists from nineteen different countries competed, their place on the program decided by lot. The date for Van's initial performance during the first round was April 2, 1958, when he played a *Prelude* and *Fugue* from Bach's *Well-Tempered Clavier*, the *C major Sonata* by Mozart (K. 330), the *Theme and Variations* of Tchaikovsky (op. 19), and some shorter pieces by Chopin, Scriabin, Liszt, and Rachmaninoff. He created a furor. He passed on easily from semifinals to the finals, all the time completely capturing the enthusiasm of his listeners. By the time he was scheduled to appear at the finals, he had become the darling of Moscow.

Everybody, it appeared, was talking about this amazing virtuoso.

Six pianists survived the finals. Each was required to play the Tchaikovsky *First Piano Concerto*, Rachmaninoff's *Third Piano Concerto*, and a *Rondo*, the last written expressly for the contest by the Soviet composer, Dimitri Kabalevsky. Cliburn was the first of the finalists to be heard. All Moscow, it seemed, tried to gain admission to the concert auditorium, where the atmosphere was charged with electric anticipation. When Cliburn completed the Tchaikovsky *Concerto*, the audience rose and cheered. After the Rachmaninoff *Concerto* enthusiasm developed into an uproar, in which even the orchestra musicians joined. Backstage Emil Gilels—himself a formidable pianist—gave Van Cliburn a giant hug. Meanwhile in the auditorium the audience was shouting in measured cadences: "First Prize—First Prize"—this, in spite of the fact that the other five finalists had yet to be heard. The most curious part of the demonstration was the fact that even the jurors were joining in the ovation—completely forgetting they were supposed to be impartial, at least until the contest was over.

Over the weekend rumors began circulating around Moscow that Van Cliburn had won. The sixteen jurors were meeting for the decision on Sunday evening, April 13, with their announcement due to be made public the following morning. But already early Sunday evening word spread all over the city that Van Cliburn's victory would be by a unanimous vote. Van Cliburn was dining with some of his friends at the Hotel Peking when a messenger rushed in, late Sunday evening, to tell him, "off the record," that he was the winner. Van Cliburn immediately made a beeline for a telephone in an effort to put a call through to his mother in Texas. By the time the wires were finally cleared between the Soviet Union and the United States he was told by his mother that she had already been congratulated via long-distance telephone by a representative of the Columbia Broadcasting System; that already the minister in Kilgore had informed his congregation of the good news at the church service. The official announcement in Moscow was still several hours off—but the news of Cliburn's victory had traveled halfway around the world with the speed of light.

And the next morning it was official. "Van Cliburn, a twenty-three-year-old American, has won the first prize in the Soviet Union's international Tchaikovsky piano competition," reported Max Frankel on the front page of *The New York Times*. "Mr. Cliburn . . . triumphed in what had been regarded as a contest of extremely high standards."

In Moscow Van Cliburn was rapidly being sucked into the quagmire of frenzied activities. Interviews had to be given to the representatives of the world's leading newspapers and journals; photographs had to be taken; he had to make appearances in front of the television cameras; a special concert had to be arranged on April 14 for the highest echelon of Soviet government officials, including Premier Khrushchev, Marshal Voroshilov, and First Deputy Premier Mikoyan; a special reception was held in his honor at the Kremlin where he received Premier Khrushchev's personal congratulations—a Russian embrace and kisses on the cheeks; the acceptance ceremony involved not only his appearance but also a performance at the piano; special concerts had to be given within a short period of time in Moscow, Leningrad, Riga, Kiev, Minsk—as well as over radio and television; festive performances of opera and ballet had to be attended as guest of honor.

Russia took Van Cliburn to its heart as it had no foreigner in recent memory. Tickets to each of his concerts could not be bought at any price; they disappeared as soon as they were made available. At the end of each performance those who had been influential enough or lucky enough to have gained admission put on a demonstration that often lasted half an hour. Wherever he went, Cliburn was overwhelmed with adulation. Whatever he said and did were duly recorded in the newspapers, almost as if he were a Soviet space hero recently returned from the stratosphere. From all over the country, from the humble as well as from the powerful, came gifts: recordings, published music, books, pictures, woodcuts, medallions, tea sets, samovars, caviar, vodka.

A month later, in the United States, the Russian furor was repeated American-style, with ticker-tape parades, gala dinners, a personal meeting with President Eisenhower at the White House, interviews, television appearances, and cover stories in national circulation magazines (including *Time*). The only question now remaining was: With all this buildup, how could Van Cliburn possibly live up to expectations? How could any performance prove anything but anticlimactic after this furor?

The answer came at his first American concert following the Soviet competition—at Carnegie Hall on May 19, 1958, when he repeated the very same progam with which he had won the Moscow contest. (Even the conductor was the same—Kiril P. Kondrashin—flown in from Moscow for this and subsequent appearances with Cliburn.) And the answer came loud and clear, without subterfuge or equivocation. "Both those who have backed him in this country and the Russians were right," reported Ross Parmenter in *The New York Times*. "He is a major talent."

23

Enough time has elapsed since 1958 for us to know with finality that Van Cliburn deserved not only the award but also the ovations and accolades that followed. Today Van Cliburn is one of the greatest box-office attractions in the concert world. He gets more engagements than he can fill in a highly active and ambulatory season. He commands in the neighborhood of $5,000 an appearance and averages about $350,000 a year. His periodic returns to the Soviet Union generate the same kind of demonstrations and excitement that first met him in that country. His recordings continue to be best sellers. In short, he is one of the elect of the concert world. If further proof were needed of this fact it comes from the number of times his name is now summoned to represent the elite among pianists. This happened in the popular song, "Specialization," by Sammy Cahn and James Van Heusen, which Marilyn Monroe introduced in the motion picture *Let's Fall in Love*. It happened again in the motion picture starring Peter Sellers, *The World of Henry Orient*. In each instance the name of Van Cliburn was used to indicate the highest realms of success in piano playing.

If Van Cliburn has thus soared to the top of his profession as a box-office draw it is no longer because of the extraordinary circumstances that made him so famous overnight. It is, rather, because he has become an artist of first significance, one of the foremost pianists of the younger generation.

Nature endowed him with two remarkable hands, extraordinary in their strength, range, and flexibility. These make possible a formidable technique which seems to reduce even the most complex compositions to simplicity. But breathtaking though his virtuosity is, it is never purchased at the price of musical sensitivity, refinement, or delicacy when the music

24

calls for these qualities. Van Cliburn, however, remains a pianist in the grand manner, in the style of Liszt, Paderewski, or Moritz Rosenthal of yesteryear, or Artur Rubinstein and Vladimir Horowitz in our own day. Van Cliburn has the capacity to create music in a large design and on an impressive canvas, but without losing details. He has the power to magnetize an audience with the first chords he strikes, and to hold that audience spellbound not only with his playing but with the dynamism of his personality. No wonder, then, that Sviatoslav Richter—acknowledged by many to be the leading pianist in the Soviet Union—did not hesitate to describe him as a "genius," adding that this was a word "I do not use lightly about performers"; that Abram Chasins wrote, "Van is a born flaming virtuoso"; that Abram Khatchaturian, the distinguished Soviet composer, regarded him as even better than Rachmaninoff, saying "you find a virtuoso like this only once or twice a century."

There is still another reason why Van Cliburn has been able to stay on the heights. Success has turned many a young head; and success of the fabulous dimensions that fell to Van Cliburn could be calculated to be disastrous. This has not been the case with Van Cliburn. He is much as he was before he won that Russian competition—simple, almost Spartan, in most of his tastes; considerate and tactful by virtue of his exceptional sensitivity and gentleness; retiring and even self-conscious, in spite of the glare of the limelight continually focused on him. He never drinks or smokes—on principle. The pleasures that his wealth can now provide him hold little interest. He still enjoys the simple delights of his earlier years—reading, association with stimulating friends in provocative conversations, and most of all music. Until 1963 he was satisfied to live in a modest apartment near Carnegie Hall, New York City. Then, feeling the need of a haven far from the madding crowd—where he could rest or study in a quiet and withdrawn setting—he finally bought a house in Tucson, Arizona.

It is highly characteristic of the kind of person he is that being one of the most significant and successful pianists of our time is not enough for him—as far as his musical ambitions go. Once he had scaled the heights of his medium, he began looking around for a new one—and found it in conducting. He now spends a good deal of his free time memorizing symphonic scores; and occasionally he tries his wings as conductor. First he directed individual numbers with various American orchestras. Then, on July 18, 1964, he led a full program for the first time, at the Lewisohn Stadium in New York City. His concert was calculated to test the mettle of even a long-experienced conductor: Kabalevsky's *Overture to Colas Breugnon;* Rachmaninoff's *Symphonic Dances;* Prokofiev's *Third Piano Concerto,* in which he filled the dual role of piano soloist and conductor. He met the test successfully, as Raymond Ericson reported in *The New York Times:* "He conducted as he plays, always letting the music breathe and stressing the long lyric line. . . . He maneuvered the orchestra securely through the score's occasional rhythmic complexities, and at no time did he try to whip up the music simply for effect. Given further experience and better acoustical conditions, Mr. Cliburn might easily become a persuasive interpreter of the orchestral repertory congenial to him." While Van Cliburn intends to intensify his activities as a conductor in the future, he insists he will never desert his first love, the piano.

One of the main reasons Van Cliburn became the idol of the Russians in 1958 was that he was always doing the right and

26

tactful thing at the right time—without fanfare, without seeking publicity. Unannounced, he made a pilgrimage to Klin to visit Tchaikovsky's home, now a museum. He carried back to America a lilac bush (the gift of a Russian admirer) to plant on Rachmaninoff's grave in the United States. The Russians liked the way in which, in spite of his obvious physical exhaustion, Cliburn insisted on seeing, shaking hands with, and talking to whoever wished to meet him. They liked the fact that in informal sessions at the piano he seemed just as ready to play for them jazz or Gershwin as Tchaikovsky or Prokofiev.

Always deeply religious—but without ever wearing his religion on his sleeve for all to see—Cliburn insists upon turning over 20 per cent of his earnings to the Baptist Church. He was generous even when he had no money. At a time when his entire savings consisted of a little less than a thousand dollars, he did not hesitate to use that money—and at the same time to sign away some of his future earnings—to buy a new Steinway grand piano for his church in New York City, which needed it badly. He also did not hesitate to give up a $500 engagement— when $500 represented to him a minor fortune—to appear and perform free at a church banquet.

He remains astonishingly modest when we take into consideration the kudos he has won and the fantastic adulation he still commands. But he is not falsely modest. When he plays well, he knows it and acknowledges that fact—a broad smile lighting up his extremely mobile face, his eyes shining as if electrified. But he is also uncompromisingly critical of himself. Nobody needs tell him when things have not gone well at the keyboard. "Did you ever hear such playing?" he once asked a friend backstage, in obvious disgust at himself. He may be severe on other pianists in their less happy musical realizations.

27

But make no mistake about it, he is most severe on himself.

It is this capacity to evaluate himself at all times, and in full and accurate measure, that has made it possible for him to grow the way he did as an artist; and to give every promise that he will continue to grow in the future.

LEON FLEISHER

[1928–   ]

$\mathcal{D}$ESPITE ALL the hullabaloo attending the Tchaikovsky
Contest in Moscow—a hullabaloo aroused far more by political and international considerations than musical ones—the
most coveted prize for performing artists is gained not in the
Soviet Union but in Belgium. Since 1937—when it was created
by the Queen Mother Elizabeth to honor Eugène Ysaÿe, one
of Belgium's most renowed musicians, a world-famous violinist
and conductor—the Queen Elizabeth of Belgium International Music Competition in Brussels (*Concours International
Eugène Ysaÿe*) has been the ultimate arena in which young
violinists and pianists the world over have had their powers
tested. Since the time when the first of these competitions was
captured by David Oistrakh and Emil Gilels—each subsequently destined to become a supreme artist—the highest
possible standards had been set for winning competitors.

In this competition all performers appear anonymously
before a discriminating musical jury whose members represent
several different countries. The young artists are required to
play a new composition never before heard together with a
traditional concerto of the performer's own choice. The con-

test lasts several weeks until the finalists are seperated from their less-fortunate rivals. It then requires three days for the finalists to compete at the concert hall in the Brussels Palais des Beaux-Arts. The first prize is $3,000 and appearances with several European symphony orchestras.

In 1952 there were seventy-one entries from twenty-seven countries. They competed before a distinguished jury comprising thirteen world-famous musicians, including Artur Rubinstein and Robert Casadesus, the concert pianists, and Olin Downes, the music critic of *The New York Times*. The new work that year was an atonal, savagely difficult work by Raymond Chevrueille, a Belgian modernist. "Even Rubinstein and Casadesus couldn't play it," remarked some Brussels musicians. "Bartók and Prokofiev are duck soup compared to it." Yet one after another of the finalists went through this taxing work as if it were just "duck soup."

One of these finalists was Leon Fleisher, aged twenty-four. Tall (six foot one) and lanky, he looked younger than his years. Indeed, on the platform he resembled a college undergraduate far more than a concert performer—but (to judge by his sensitive face, highly expressive and intelligent brown eyes, and impressive brow) an undergraduate more interested in the debating society, college journal, and the Phi Beta Kappa key than in "proms" and football games. He gave the impression of being a typical young American—if, indeed, there is such a genre—so much so that when he sat down to the piano one almost expected to hear jazz. But once his two strong hands descended on the keyboard for the opening chords—once the muscles of that sensitive face tensed and the brow became furrowed with wrinkles—all other ideas about him vanished. This, without any doubt, was an artist.

He went through round after round of the competition with professional ease and self-assurance. (His choice of concerto was Brahms's *First in D minor*.) In the preliminary rounds his playing aroused such enthusiasm that the presiding judge had to sound a bell to silence the audience. There was a minor mishap in the final round when a piano string snapped while he was midway in the Brahms *Concerto*. But not even that unnerved him. The audience was sure that he was the winner, but had to wait two hours for the judges' decision. He was the winner, by a unanimous vote. Artur Rubinstein called him "a deep musician," adding: "There is hope for a truly great pianist." Olin Downes remarked succinctly: "He had the Dempsey punch."

In this way Fleisher became the first American ever to win the first prize in this Brussels competition. Indeed, he was also at the time the first American ever to win a major foreign competition.

The winning of the Queen Elizabeth competition separated the artist from the prodigy. Leon Fleisher was born in San Francisco on July 23, 1928. His father was a fashion designer; his mother had been a student of singing in her native Poland. When Leon was five, his older brother, Raymond, started to take piano lessons. This seeming partiality infuriated the younger child, who then and there noisily insisted that he be given equal rights where music was concerned. Leon, therefore, started piano study with Lev Shorr, under whose sympathetic instruction he made such progress that he was able to give a recital in San Francisco when he was only seven. Two years after that he appeared as a soloist with one of the local orchestras in the same city.

Artur Schnabel, one of the most highly esteemed pianists of

his time, paid San Francisco a visit when Fleisher was ten. Despite Schnabel's openly expressed prejudice to prodigies, he was finally prevailed upon to listen to Fleisher. After hearing him, Schnabel broke a long-standing rule of his never to accept anybody as a pupil younger than sixteen. In fact, he encouraged Fleisher to come to his studio at Lake Como, Italy, for an intensive period of private instruction.

Returning to the United States from Lake Como, Fleisher appeared as a soloist with the San Francisco Symphony conducted by Pierre Monteux. Although only fifteen at the time, Fleisher's success was so impressive that Monteux invited him to appear under his baton at a concert of the New York Philharmonic Orchestra on November 4, 1944—Fleisher's New York bow. This was followed by a Carnegie Hall recital less than three months later. Both appearances led critics to hail him as the most significant new pianist heard in New York in several years—a pianist already in full command of his technique and endowed with the most discriminating taste, musicianship, and style.

Fleisher made many appearances after this in recitals and as soloist with major symphony orchestras. Then, in 1950, feeling the need for further development both as a musician and a human being, he went to Paris to absorb Europe's cultural conditions and to perfect his piano performance. During this period he gave his first concerts in Europe. When he finally felt he was ready for a supreme test, he proceeded to Brussels to compete in the Queen Elizabeth competition for pianists in 1952.

In his tours through the four continents since 1954 Fleisher has become a favorite of discriminating music lovers. This is because in his playing he never stoops to conquer. He prefers

to devote himself to the profoundest works in the piano literature, works that demand from him the utmost in musicianship,
culture, and artistic penetration. He is far less interested in
those pyrotechnical creations that send off glittering fireworks
and are calculated to dazzle and then blind audiences with
brilliant flashing colors. To devote oneself to the deeper and
more meaningful compositions, and to sidestep the showpieces
so favored by audiences, is the long route an artist takes toward
success. This was the path his teacher, Artur Schnabel, had
once chosen, and this is the reason that it took so long for
Schnabel to be recognized as the master he was. But if it is the
longer course, it is also the surer one. An audience may grow
weary of pyrotechnics in time; it never grows tired of penetrating re-creations of unqualified masterworks.

It was Fleisher's musicianship, far more than his consummate
technical equipment, that has always won the praises of critics.
"Fleisher," wrote Rudolph Elie, critic of the Boston *Herald*,
"is a pianist of broad musical horizons in every way. . . . He
[has] first of all immense power, but a power always in control. . . . He [has] a most advanced sensitivity to the more
lyrical qualities of the work as well, producing a beautiful tone
of a sustained but always clear and lucid quality. More than
that, he [gets] beneath the surface to evoke an atmosphere of
the most radiant character."

What Harriet Johnson of the New York *Post* once said of
Fleisher's performance of Brahms's *Second Piano Concerto*
applies to every work to which Fleisher addresses himself. "He
had all the necessary power and technical command for the
work's gigantic structure. But, fortunately, he not only poured
himself into the mold and encompassed it, but he burst its
bonds too. Besides a determined, driving conviction there was

33

also a strong spontaneous feeling for its joyous lyricism and for its many reflective moments. . . . He had a mature conception of the music and he was able impressively to re-create it with magnitude."

As we already have had the occasion to remark, where so many other artists woo their audiences, and encourage their applause, with popular, familiar, or meretricious pieces of music, Leon Fleisher dedicates himself primarily only to that literature that makes the most exacting demands on his musical intelligence, sensibilities, and instincts. He has given world *premières* of provocative new works—for example, Leon Kirchner's *Second Piano Concerto* which the Ford Foundation had commissioned for Fleisher and whose *première* he gave in Seattle, Washington, in 1963–1964; or (for an even more esoteric public) the first performance anywhere of Alberto Ginastera's *Piano Quintet*, heard at a concert in Washington, D.C., the same season. Where other artists try to pack a hall by presenting the ever-appealing all-Chopin program, Fleisher might prefer a concert devoted entirely to Schubert, which is not good box-office. He did so in New York on March 23, 1963, to inspire one New York critic to call him then "a rare pianist who can play with such depth and with such fidelity to the inner spirit of the composer's music." Other artists might strive for best-selling recording albums by turning to such war horses as the Tchaikovsky *First Piano Concerto* or the Rachmaninoff *Second Piano Concerto*. Fleisher is ready to gamble with releases which beckon to a more sophisticated public: Paul Hindemith's *The Four Temperaments* and *Trauermusik;* Brahm's *Variations on a Theme of Handel;* Karl Maria von Weber's unfamiliar *E minor Piano Sonata;* an album of contemporary American compositions for the piano. It was because the recording director of Epic Records was fully aware of his deep and discerning gift in the interpretation of the profoundest works in the repertory that, in 1961, Fleisher was selected to put on disks all the five Beethoven piano concertos, supported by the Cleveland Orchestra under George Szell. Fleisher is the first pianist of his generation to record all five of Beethoven's piano concertos. "This," said *The New York Times* in review, "is a project usually reserved for artists of the maturity of Bachaus, Rubinstein, Serkin, and Kempff. But Mr. Fleisher can hold his head high among the gray eminence, for his performances here add up to a distinguished, remarkable achievement."

Being chosen to record the five Beethoven piano concertos with the Cleveland Orchestra is proof of the high station Fleisher has by now acquired in the music world. Equally convincing is the testimony that came in 1958 when Fleisher was selected to play at two of Europe's most highly regarded music festivals, one in Berlin and the other in Salzburg; also when during the same year President Eisenhower invited him to perform at the White House during a state dinner for King Baudouin of the Belgians.

Leon Fleisher makes his home in Baltimore, Maryland, the home town of his wife, Rikki Rosenthal. They have one child, a daughter (though by a previous marriage Fleisher has three other children, two girls and a boy). Between concert tours Fleisher spends all of his time with his family in Baltimore, occupying himself with such diversions as playing ping-pong, bridge, and arranging barbecues for close friends. Freed from the pressures of concertizing, Fleisher leads what he calls "the most sedentary life imaginable." Part of his time in Baltimore is occupied with his teaching chores at the Peabody Conservatory. He reveals, with a chuckle, that the only reason he took on this job in the first place was that he wanted to buy a house, and the bank would not give him a mortgage unless he had a regular salaried post. Teaching young, gifted pianists, however, has since become a significant phase of Fleisher's musical life. He remembers only too well the debt he owes to Schnabel. He would like to repay that debt by passing on the Schnabel heritage to the next generation of gifted young pianists.

GARY GRAFFMAN

[1918–   ]

BYRON JANIS

[1928–   ]

AMONG THE other Amercian concert pianists of the younger generation who are now held in high esteem throughout the world of music are Gary Graffman and Byron Janis. The one— Gary Graffman—is in the image of those artists whom Europe had once nurtured to greatness and whom it has always venerated—pianists such as Artur Schnabel and Wilhelm Bachaus. Like them Graffman is the total musician, the artist all of one piece. Technique, musicianship, personality, insight are all so fully integrated that it is impossible to say which of these traits one admires most in him. With a minimum of personal display, with a total absence of eccentricities or idiosyncrasies, he addresses himself to a masterwork with the humility of a high priest serving his religion.

Byron Janis, the other, is more in the image of his one-time teacher, Vladimir Horowitz. Horowitz is probably the greatest technician the keyboard has known in our times. Beautiful sounds are coordinated with electrifying colors and effects. "Unparalleled tension and sonority coupled to one of the most flawless techniques in piano history"—this is the way Harold C. Schonberg described Horowitz in his book *The Great Pianists*. This does not mean that taste, artistry, musicianship are lacking. Not by any means. But it does mean that while some artists whisper to their audience magical secrets, others speak out and overwhelm them with thunder and passion. Byron Janis belongs in the latter category.

Gary Graffman preceded Van Cliburn and Leon Fleisher in using a major competition as the launching pad from which to catapult to success. But with Graffman the competition was of American rather than European origin; and with Graffman (unlike Cliburn) that flight to success did not come with the instantaneous explosion of jet propulsion, but in a slow and gradual ascent. Fame came to Graffman only after he had fully matured as a human being; after he had extended his studies and intellectual stimulations into fields other than music; after he had had an opportunity to master a repertory and make it a reflection of his own aesthetic experiences. Once that evolution had taken place—and it took several years for this to happen—nothing could keep Graffman from scaling the peaks and staying there.

Today Graffman is something of a favorite with the world's great symphony orchestras. He has appeared more than twenty times each with the Boston Symphony and with the Liverpool Philharmonic; he was the only soloist with the Philharmonia Orchestra of London in a Brahms festival conducted by Otto Klemperer; he participated with the New York Philharmonic in the opening ceremonies of Philharmonic Hall at Lincoln Center in 1962. He has recorded some of the greatest concertos in the repertory with the Chicago Orchestra (under Walter Hendl), the Boston Symphony (under Charles Munch), the New York Philharmonic (under Leonard Bernstein), and the San Francisco Orchestra (under Josef Krips).

Graffman has made more than ten tours of Europe, has appeared at least once in every other area of the world including the Far East. "Of all the brilliant young pianists produced by the United States during the past ten years, Gary Graffman is perhaps the most impressive," said the critic of the London *Daily Telegraph*. The critic of the *Morgenpost* in Berlin wrote: "Gary Graffman undoubtedly belongs to the top rank of pianists." When Graffman played in Cape Town, its leading newspaper—the *Times*—commented: "It was a red-letter day." The *Christian Science Monitor* in Boston summed up his significance by saying: "He is a pianist to be ranked among the great of our time."

He is American-born and American-trained, but of Russian background. His father, Vladimir, had been a violin pupil of Leopold Auer at the St. Petersburg Conservatory. Subsequently Vladimir Graffman assumed the post of director at the Omk Conservatory in Siberia. After coming to the United States, he served as concertmaster of the Minneapolis Symphony. He then settled down in New York as one of its most successful violin teachers, for a while as Leopold Auer's first assistant.

Gary Graffman was born in New York City, on October 14, 1918. When he was three, he received the gift of a miniature violin with which his father tried to teach him. When the child had difficulty in handling that instrument, the father decided to teach him the piano instead. Gary's progress soon convinced the father to turn him over to the more experienced instruction of Mrs. Harold Morris. It was not long before Gary,

39

now aged seven, auditioned at the Curtis Institute of Music in Philadelphia where he gave such a prodigal demonstration that he was given a ten-year scholarship with Mme. Isabella Vengerova, the Institute's leading piano teacher. Only one year after that the boy was heard as soloist with the Philadelphia Symphonette, Fabien Sevitzky conducting. Sevitzky was sufficiently impressed with this eleven-year-old pianist to invite him to appear with the Indianapolis Symphony. This was followed by Graffman's impressive debut at Town Hall, New York City, which led the critic of *The New York Times* to say that he played "with a searching sense of style and an almost uncanny amount of musical understanding and poetry for a child of his years."

Profitable offers for concert appearances—offers even from Hollywood to play in the movies—were a lure to which Graffman's parents refused to succumb. With rare wisdom, they dismissed an easy success. Gary was permitted to make only intermittent appearances as a part of his over-all training. Otherwise he confined himself to his music studies at the Curtis Institute; to his academic education at the Columbia Grammar School in New York City; to the normal pursuits of a healthy American boy, including baseball and football, refusing on any account to pamper his precious hands.

In 1946 he was graduated from both the Curtis Institute and the Columbia Grammar School. Although he enrolled for further academic education at Columbia University (again on a scholarship), he now stood ready to advance his concert career.

Meanwhile, soon after the death of Serge Rachmaninoff in 1943, a fund had been created to honor that famous Russian composer and pianist through the presentation of awards to

deserving performers and composers. The first such competition was for native-born or naturalized pianists between the
ages of seventeen and twenty-eight. The winner was to receive
a recording contract with RCA-Victor, a national tour, and
appearances with major symphony orchestras.

The country was divided into seven regions, the winner from
each to compete with one another for the grand prize. So high
were the standards that only in Philadelphia was a pianist found
worthy of capturing a regional award. He was Gary Graffman.
Since there was nobody to compete with him for it, the first
prize was canceled. On the other hand, Gary Graffman could
not be ignored. Having won his part in the competition, he
became the recipient of a special award. This entitled him to
appear with the Philadelphia Orchestra on March 28, 1947,
in a performance of Rachmaninoff's *Second Piano Concerto*,
Eugene Ormandy conducting. One day later Graffman's
performance of this concerto, with the same orchestra and
conductor, was broadcast over the facilities of the Columbia
Broadcasting System from coast to coast.

The enthusiastic reaction to these two appearances led to
recitals in Philadelphia, Washington, Baltimore, and finally
New York City. One season later Graffman received first prize
in the Leventritt Award which enabled him to play with the
New York Philharmonic under Leonard Bernstein, the Cleveland Orchestra under George Szell, and the Buffalo Philharmonic under William Sternberg. Although he was now under
the managment of Columbia Artists, and though extended
tours were now being planned for him, Gary Graffman wisely
refused to allow the demands of the concert stage to infringe
upon and impose limitations on his cultural growth. In 1950
he traveled and studied in Italy on a Fulbright Fellowship. In

1951 he established a one-year residence in Paris for further cultural development.

Only when he felt he had reached maturity both as a human being and as a musician did Graffman finally begin to concentrate completely on advancing his concert career. He toured with the Little Orchestra Society in the spring of 1953 when he was heard in five different concertos. In the summer of 1955 he made his first tour of South America. His first full-scale tour of Europe, launched in the fall of 1956, was set into motion with a remarkable debut in London when he presented Prokofiev's *Third Piano Concerto* with the London Philharmonic. In 1958–1959 a six-month world tour enhanced his international stature.

Gary Graffman is of medium height and stocky in build. At first glance he looks more like a college teacher or a research scientist than a concert pianist. An expressive face is a mirror that continually betrays his changing moods. As Howard Klein said, his facial expressions "seem to change abruptly from a brooding thoughtfulness to a smiling buoyancy with almost no stages in between."

When he is not touring Graffman lives in an apartment on Fifty-seventh Street in New York City (near Carnegie Hall), with his wife Naomi, whom he married in 1952 while she was studying music seriously with Wallingford Riegger and Stefan Wolpe. She now combines her interest in music with painting. Inveterate collectors, the Graffmans have cluttered their apartment with all sorts of curiosities gathered during their extensive tours around the world: terra-cotta figures from the Philippines; a seventeenth-century ikon purchased in a covered bazaar in Istanbul; a pierced, illuminated leather screen picked up in Bangkok; a six-foot Hawaiian tiki carved from a fern stump.

There is something else the Graffmans like to collect—recipes from all over the world. They are both highly creative in the kitchen, their specialties including such exotic dishes as marinated shish-kebab or Javanese pork sautés.

Beyond collecting, Graffman's interests outside music include books (he is an omniverous reader) and sight-seeing in foreign lands. He is also keenly aware of the social and political problems of the day; he does not hide himself in an ivory tower. Early in 1964 he was involved in one of these social problems to become front-page news. On Febuary 27 he was scheduled to play under the auspices of the Community Concerts in Jackson, Mississippi, a city that followed a strict segregation policy. Informed that two Negro students were arrested for trying to gain admission to this concert, Graffman sat up and took notice of his own place in the racial struggle. His first impulse was to turn over the proceeds from this concert to the NAACP. But he soon came to realize that his protest against segregation would be even stronger if he refused to appear in any auditorium that excluded Negroes. His widely publicized cancellation of the Jackson concert started a chain reaction that led many other famous artists to announce at once that they would no longer give concerts in segregated auditoriums.

The temptation to describe Byron Janis as "a young Vladimir Horowitz" comes, of course, first and foremost, from the fact that for three years Janis was Vladimir Horowitz's pupil—Horowitz's *only* pupil as a matter of fact. Janis now explains that Horowitz taught him all the possibilities of the piano and how to realize them scientifically not only through a thorough understanding of the instrument but also through digital exercises calculated to develop Janis's hands in the way

43

best suited to their anatomy. Horowitz concentrated on technical problems because he believed implicitly that a gifted pianist must be allowed to develop artistically in his own way. It is for this reason that study with Horowitz concentrated more on technique and piano sound than on structural or stylistic analysis.

Studying with Horowitz brought rewards to Janis through one of the most formidable techniques to be encountered among the younger pianists, a technique that can truly be described as "Horowitzian." But that study also exacted a heavy toll from Janis. If it took him three years to acquire a Horowitz-like command of the keyboard, and to be able to produce Horowitz-like sonorities and dynamics, it took Janis another few years after that to liberate himself from Horowitz's influence. Soon after his lessons had permanently ended (Janis never had another teacher), he realized that he was imitating his teacher far too often, that he was studiously trying to sound like Horowitz. He therefore now needed a number of years of additional work all by himself to reach for and acquire his own artistic identity. Here is the way he put it to an interviewer for *Musical America*: "The important thing is to say something artistically that is *you*—to learn to find yourself through making mistakes that are *your* mistakes. There are many ways of performing a given work, but the artist must be convinced that *his* way is right. This is what gives authority to his performance." Having finally found his own way (however much it may originally have been guided and directed by Horowitz), Byron Janis was able to acquire his own place in music—not as a "second Horowitz" but as a "first Byron Janis."

He was born in McKeesport, Pennsylvania, on March 24, 1928. While he was going to kindergarten, his teacher dis-

44

covered that he displayed unusual interest whenever the children sang songs; also that while playing with a toy xylophone he disclosed that he had perfect pitch. The teacher urged Janis's parents to begin teaching him music formally. Piano study, then, was begun when Byron was five; four years later the nine-year-old prodigy gave a recital in one of Pittsburgh's leading concert halls.

Among those in the audience at that concert was Josef Lhevinne, in his time a world-famous virtuoso, since then a hardly less celebrated piano teacher. Lhevinne suggested that Byron Janis be brought to New York and that he study the piano with Adele Marcus at the Chatham School of Music in Greenwich Village. In New York Janis combined this piano study with lessons in composition and harmony, and with an academic education at the Columbia Grammar School.

The director of the Chatham Music School was Samuel Chotzinoff, who combined this post with that of music director of the National Broadcasting Company. Chotzinoff soon became aware of Byron Janis's immense talent. He arranged for the fifteen-year-old boy to appear as soloist with the NBC Symphony Orchestra over the NBC network (Frank Black conducting), and to give a number of concerts over the air waves.

When Adele Marcus left the Chatham School in New York to become a member of the faculty at the Hockaday Music School in Dallas, Texas, Janis followed her. At the same time he gave a number of concerts outside Texas. One of these, in 1943, was an appearance with the Pittsburgh Symphony, the occasion upon which Vladimir Horowitz had an opportunity to hear him play. Horowitz was so impressed that he persuaded Janis to devote the next few years in concentrated study under

45

his personal supervision. This was the first time that Horowitz had ever made such an offer to a young musician. Janis, naturally, eagerly accepted.

After completing a three-year period of study with Horowitz, and a briefer period of adjustment and self-discovery, Janis stood ready to resume his concert career. He appeared throughout the United States both in recitals and as soloist with principal orchestras. On October 29, 1948, he made his New York debut with a recital at Carnegie Hall that led Olin Downes, the critic of *The New York Times*, to write: "Not for a long time has this writer heard such a talent." A few months after that, as soloist with the New York Philharmonic in George Gershwin's *Piano Concerto in F*, Janis inspired Irving Kolodin to say in the New York *Sun:* "He is certainly the finest pianist we have ever heard in this score." And two years later (eloquent evidence of Janis's continual growth) the critic of the *New York Herald Tribune* remarked: "There is nothing in the literature for the piano which lies beyond the reach of his technical powers."

His first tour of South America took place in 1948; that of Europe began in 1952 with five concerts with the Concertgebouw Orchestra of Amsterdam. In 1958 Janis was called upon to initiate the American Festival Week at the World's Fair in Brussels. In 1961, to celebrate the one hundred and fiftieth anniversary of the birth of Franz Liszt, he performed both Liszt's piano concertos on a single program with the Boston Symphony Orchestra in the United States and with the Paris Conservatory Orchestra in France. In 1961 Janis also became the first American pianist to tour the Soviet Union since Van Cliburn—sent there by the State Department. His reception by the Soviet music lovers was described by *The New York*

Times as "overwhelming . . . men and women in the audience wept." He returned to the Soviet Union in the spring of 1962 at the invitation of the Soviet Ministry of Culture. After he had performed three concertos in a single evening with the Moscow State Symphony, its conductor, Kiril Kondrashin, said: "I have now heard a pianist who can play three utterly different concertos with a perfect sense of style. He is one of the greatest pianists of the age." During this Soviet visit Janis earned the additional distinction of making the first American recordings ever permitted in the Soviet Union, for the Mercury label. One of these—that of Prokofiev's *Third Piano Concerto*—received the French Grand Prix as the best classical recording of 1963, the highest honor the European recording industry can bestow.

Janis's home is where he hangs his hat. Because of his extensive travels each year around the world, Janis looks upon the various hotel rooms of the different cities he visits as home—and so do his wife and son, who often accompany him. His wife is the former June Dickson Wright, a London girl, daughter of the senior surgeon of St. Mary's Hospital. They were married in 1953, and on March 20, 1955, a son named Stefan was born to them.

Janis is a sports enthusiast, but as a participant he confines himself exclusively to ping-pong and badminton, and to driving sports cars. Of his other nonmusical interests, he is most partial to the movies and to good food and wines.

GLENN GOULD

[1932-   ]

$\mathcal{G}$LENN GOULD's strange mannerisms and eccentricities on the stage sometimes make it difficult to remember that he is one of the most scholarly and penetrating interpreters of piano literature today; that he is, as Alfred Frankenstein, the distinguished critic in San Francisco, described him, the "foremost pianist this continent has produced in recent decades." Gould is an interpreter of Bach's keyboard music with few rivals. He knows how to make the modern piano approximate Bach's clavier—feeling strongly, as he does, that the sounds that Bach heard in his mind's ear are not those usually being realized on the present-day Steinway or Baldwin. Gould knows how to make Bach's ornamentations grow naturally out of the organism of the melody instead of serving merely as superfluous trimmings. He can make a contrapuntal texture, however complex, crystal clear. And he has an aristocratic feeling for baroque style, baroque being that period in music history of which Bach was the summit. "He plays Bach," wrote Professor Heinrich Neuhaus in the Soviet publication *Culture and Life*, "as if he were one of the pupils of the Thomaskirche. . . . His performance is of extraordinary significance in having, as it were, bridged the distance between Bach and our own days." In Vienna the critics said of him: "We do not know of anyone who can equal him in the interpretation of the great master [Bach]" and "Glenn Gould is possessed by Bach, under [whose fingers] beats the great sensitive heart of Bach."

Yet unlike so many other Bach authorities, Gould does not live exclusively in the seventeenth and eighteenth centuries. He is also a child of his own times, one of the leading exponents of contemporary keyboard literature on the concert stage. He plays the works of such atonalists as Alban Berg and Arnold Schoenberg or such neoclassicists as Paul Hindemith with equal authority. Both as pianist and as a conductor he has often presented programs devoted exclusively to modern music which (as one reviewer on *The New York Times* remarked) "looked awful . . . on paper" but which turned out through his presentations to be an "absorbing experience, largely because Mr. Gould is as gifted a musical thinker as he is a pianist." Gould also happens to be a student of jazz, having frequently appeared in concerts with intimate jazz groups, both as a performer and a composer.

Nevertheless, his peculiar behavior on the concert stage unfortunately tends to deflect the attention of audiences from his playing to himself. When he first comes out on the platform he looks gaunt and ascetic, like some high priest about to perform a ritual. Soon he will begin to fuss endlessly with his piano chair (he uses only a chair of his own design), first to the amusement, then to the exasperation, of the audience. Once, as soloist with the Cleveland Orchestra, he wasted more than half an hour of rehearsal time turning the screws of his chair, now adjusting the seat higher, now lower, and apparently unable to arrive at a comfortable position. Finally, the usually even-tempered conductor, George Szell, erupted into a fury, showered Gould with fiery expletives, then stalked off the stage, vowing never again to conduct for Gould. When Gould next appeared with his orchestra, an associate conductor had to take over the baton. Hearing Gould's performance of Beethoven's *Second Piano Concerto*, Szell remarked: "No doubt about it—that nut is a genius."

Gould is likely to put on a distracting show while playing. Now he conducts expansively when either hand or both hands are temporarily idle. Now he hums and sings audibly with the music. Now he breathes heavily. Now he mutters all sorts of comments about the quality of his performance. Some writers have recalled that half a century ago or more there was another formidable concert pianist also given to such unorthodox demonstrations. His name was Vladimir de Pachmann. Though a truly extraordinary performer (particularly of Chopin), De Pachmann used to attract audiences into the concert hall more to witness his shenanigans than to hear him play. But there was (truth to tell) a good deal of the charlatan in De Pachmann, a good deal of the studied showman, and a good deal of Peck's bad boy. Gould, on the other hand, is exclusively a victim of emotions and compulsions he simply cannot control.

Because of his pronounced idiosyncrasies, Gould is probably the only living concert artist whose greatness is projected more faithfully on phonograph records than in live performances. After all, when one listens to a Gould recording one hears the music and the music alone—without any of the eccentric preliminaries that so infuriate the recording engineers who have to deal with him in the flesh. Here is how *Time* magazine described one of Gould's rather unusual recording sessions, back in 1955: "The frail-looking young pianist walked into the recording studio one day last June wearing beret, coat, muffler, and gloves, carrying two large bottles of spring water to drink, five small bottles of pills, and his own piano chair. Before he started to play he soaked his hands and arms in hot water. Then he began a week's stint. . . . Sometimes he sang as he played, and when he finished a 'take' that particularly pleased him, he jumped up with a gleeful 'Wow!' But when a piano note sagged by a hair, a tuner was called instantly. And when the pianist made the same mistake three times, he announced he must be suffering from a mental block."

Unhappy in front of a live audience—and convinced that the modern huge concert hall is just not the place to give a piano recital—Gould gives of his best in his recording sessions. As *Time* reported a second time, now in 1964: "With a piano on which the stroke of each key has been shortened a fraction of an inch to make its action more like that of a harpsichord, Gould works tirelessly at recording sessions, positioning the microphone so close to the piano that his constant contrapuntal humming sometimes comes through on records. . . . His concert career has been made mainly notorious for flashes of eccentricity . . . while his recording career has been little short of genius."

It was, as a matter of fact, with a recording—and not with a public concert—that Gould's name and artistry first flashed across the musical horizon like blinding lightning. This happened in 1956. Then completely unknown to the music world at large, his first recording for Columbia—Bach's *Goldberg Variations*—was released without any fanfare of publicity bugles. The recording proved a sensation. The twentieth-century concert world has known the distinguished work of many a Bach specialist and many an impressive interpretation

52

of the *Goldberg Variations* (one of Bach's most monumental works for the keyboard)—from Harold Samuel to Rosalyn Tureck, from Wanda Landowska to Ralph Kirkpatrick. But even in comparison with such performances Gould's came as a kind of revelation. Irving Kolodin, the music critic of the *Saturday Review* and one of the keenest evaluators of recorded music, wrote: "Here, unquestionably, is Something: a young pianist who can take such a seemingly mechanical sequence as Bach's elaborations . . . and make an absorbing, wholly interesting experience of it. . . . Gould not only has the finger discipline that can be taught, but also the kind of darting finesse that cannot. In other words, along with learning the mechanics of his instrument thoroughly, Gould has been imbued with a considerable sense of what to do with them."

Since 1956 Gould has recorded a good deal of Bach's keyboard music, including the *Well-Tempered Clavier*, the *Art of the Fugue*, the *Partitas*, two concertos with orchestra, the solo *Italian Concerto*. He has also recorded major works by Mozart, Haydn, and Brahms of centuries past; of Schoenberg, Ernest Krenek, and Alban Berg from our own times. The wide range of his re-creative talent and the profundity of his musical insight are therefore available for home consumption.

Glenn Gould is a Canadian, having been born in Toronto on September 25, 1932. A prodigy to whom the making of music always came as naturally as breathing, he was entered in the Toronto Conservatory while he was still a child. There he studied piano with Albert Guerrero and composition with Leo Smith. He was graduated from the Conservatory when he was only twelve—the youngest musician to do so in the history of the institution. At the same time he received the highest honors the Conservatory could bestow, not only in piano playing but also in composition.

On January 14, 1947, he made his concert debut in Toronto by performing the *Fourth Piano Concerto* of Beethoven with the Toronto Symphony, Ernest MacMillan conducting. Critics pronounced him at once the mature, fully-developed artist— yet Gould at the time was not yet fifteen years old.

It took seven years for Gould to be heard outside Canada. On January 2, 1955, Gould made his debut in the United States with a concert in Washington, D.C. "We know of no pianist anything like him of any age," said Paul Hume in the Washington *Post*. A New York recital followed one week later. Although the critics sat up and took notice, it was only through his recording of Bach's *Goldberg Variations*, released in January 1956, that the general music public in America first became aware of the presence of an uncommon artist.

His first coast-to-coast American tour in 1956–1957 fully confirmed the profound impression made by his first recording. "He is a genius . . . one of the greatest artists in the world," was the unequivocal statement of Arthur Darasch of the Cincinnati *Inquirer*. Then came his bow in Europe with three appearances with the Berlin Philharmonic conducted by Herbert von Karajan. The Berlin musical community, one of the most discriminating in Europe, buzzed with excitement. "Gould plays," said Berlin's most eminent music critic, H. H. Stuckenschmidt, "as if possessed physically by a thousand passions, a young man in the strange way of a trance, an artist on the edge of dream and reality. His technical abilities are fabulous; the fluency in both hands, the manifold dynamics, and the many colors of his touch represent a degree of mastery which I have not come across since the time of Busoni."

That May Gould became the first North American artist to

54

play in the Soviet Union. He gave eight concerts in Moscow and Leningrad within a two-week period. All performances were completely sold out. Six extra policeman had to be called to keep in check the crowds who could not gain admission. Standees occupied every available space in the hall, including the aisles, and at one performance precedence in the Soviet Union was broken when a hundred people were allowed to sit on the stage. *Pravda* referred to his concerts as "a bright and shining event in the musical world"; the Soviet composer, Vadim Salmanov, described his playing as "veritable sorcery."

When, in 1958, Gould had completed a comprehensive sweep of Europe, he paid his first visit to Israel. Here, too, the praises knew no limits. "Such playing," said the critic of *Haaretz*, "moves the listener to the depths of his soul by its almost religious expression. We have never heard anything like it in one of our concerts. . . . He is a musical sensation."

Gould's expansive musical intellectualism makes it impossible for him to confine himself exclusively to the keyboard. On July 9, 1956—when an entire program was assigned to him at the Second Annual Music Festival at Stratford, Ontario—he was heard not only as a pianist, but also as a conductor and composer. Since then he has become the codirector of this, one of Canada's most important festivals, and is largely responsible for its rapid growth as one of the greatest cultural events in North America. As a composer, he has written an excellent string quartet which has been recorded by Columbia. Gould has also distinguished himself as a program annotator; as a writer on musical subjects; as a lecturer (notably on subjects like the "Piano Sonata" or "Modern Music") at universities; and as a television personality. Sometimes dubbed "Canada's Leonard Bernstein," Gould has been featured in several full-hour television "spectaculars" as narrator, performer, and author of the scripts, in a variety of themes ranging from such masters as Bach and Beethoven to such subjects as the fugue and modern music.

ISAAC STERN

[1920–   ]

W HEN ISAAC STERN, violinist, toured the Soviet Union for the first time in 1956, he became the first American concert performer to play in that country in more than a decade, and the first ever to broadcast over the Soviet television. Thus he was responsible for reversing the tide of musical-performance history, or, to borrow a cliché, to carry coals to Newcastle. Since the turn of the twentieth century Russia had been the cradle of violin virtuosity, the country from which came most of the violinists America revered highly through the years: Mischa Elman, Jascha Heifetz, Nathan Milstein, Toscha Seidel, Mishel Piastro, Mischa Mischakoff, Efrem Zimbalist, to name just a representative few. Most of them had been pupils of Leopold Auer, one of the greatest violin teachers of all time, whose classes at the St. Petersburg Conservatory were the nursery where many a genius of the violin was raised then sent off fully equipped in every detail of performance to conquer the music world. The proliferation of Russian violinists on the American concert scene in the 1910's and 1920's once led George and Ira Gershwin to write a comedy number with which they used to delight their friends at parties. It was called

"Mischa, Jascha, Toscha, Sascha." The closing lines of the opening verse read: "When we began, Our notes were sour, Until a man (Professor Auer), Set out to show us, one and all, How we could pack them in, in Carnegie Hall."

Russian violinists coming to America, therefore, was the rule. But American violinists going to Russia, until Isaac Stern went in 1956, was something else again. Appearing in Russia was possibly the severest test to which a young American violinist could subject himself. It was to be expected that a country that had produced Heifetz and Milstein and Elman should be hypersensitive about its achievements in violin playing, and should be hypercritical of foreign competition.

Isaac Stern met that test. His performances in Moscow, Leningrad, Kiev, Tiflis, Baku, and Ervan between May 3 and June 1, 1956 (and over Soviet television) created a furor. The audiences showered him with audible and visible signs of adulation, standing ovations, flowers, gifts. The critics described his performances as violin playing *in excelsis*. They had no hesitancy in saying that in Stern America had produced a violinist worthy to rank with the Russian immortals.

Stern made a second tour of the Soviet Union in 1960, a critical time that probably was an even severer test of his appeal and popularity. This, you may recall, was the period when the V-2 flight over the Soviet Union disrupted the impending Soviet-American summit conference in Paris between President Eisenhower and Premier Khrushchev. Hostility to America and Americans was fanned into hot flame by the Soviet press and by public statements of the leaders. Yet Stern had only to appear on the concert stage and put fiddle to chin for the Soviet music audiences to forget international frictions completely in the presence of exalted music making.

58

At that there is a tenuous tie between Isaac Stern and the So- viet Union. Although he is an American citizen, had in fact lived in the United States from the time he was ten months old, and had received all his training on the violin from Amer- ican teachers, Isaac Stern *did* come from Russian parentage, and indeed had been born in the Soviet Union. The date was July 21, 1920; the place, the little town of Kriminiesz near the Polish border. His mother had studied voice at the St. Peters- burg Conservatory. His father, an artist, was an amateur musi- cian and a dedicated music lover.

As an infant Isaac Stern was brought by his family to the United States to find a permanent home in San Francisco. At the age of six he began taking piano lessons, showing little enthusiasm for either music or the instrument, and for two years struggling along with his exercises the way any other musical novice might. He was on the verge of giving up music for good when one day, in his eighth year, he heard a youngster across the street practising the violin. The sounds fascinated him. Forthwith he begged his parents for violin lessons. His native musical instincts now blossomed with a local teacher. Then, at ten, with funds provided by a patron from San Fran- cisco's swank Pacific Avenue, Isaac was enrolled in the San Francisco Conservatory. One year later he made his first public appearance—as soloist, no less, with the San Francisco Sym- phony Orchestra, Pierre Monteux conducting. For about a year after that he studied with Louis Persinger in New York City. Then, back once again in San Francisco, Stern was taken on by Naoum Blinder, the concertmaster of the San Francisco Symphony. "Blinder," Stern later recalled, "taught me how to teach myself—the sign of a really good teacher." Blinder was concerned mainly with guiding the young musician through the subtleties of the violin repertory and in seeking out the inmost meanings of a piece of music. As for technique, Stern admits he has been mostly self-taught, a skill acquired through many years of experimentation, of trial and error, of the most painstaking self-application to and solution of each given problem. For that matter, even his artistic growth has been mostly of a self-learning process, a gradual and consistent development through the years that can come only through the continual study of scores, the re-examination of one's musical ideas, the indefatigable search for new ways to say old things.

While Stern's concert career predates World War II, his success and his placement with the elite of the concert world are a postwar development. He gave his first recital in New York City as far back as October 12, 1937. His playing inspired some praise but many reservations as well. The critics liked his tone but found fault with his intonation; praised his enthusiasm but pointed to his immaturity. "He has the makings of a fine player," one critic said, "but he should watch himself and listen carefully to his colleagues." The critic of the *Herald Tribune* remarked: "Following a normal and judicious course of development he should become an artist of exceptional consequence." What was Stern's reaction to this debut? "I was too old to be a prodigy and too young to be mistaken for a finished artist."

That concert convinced Stern that he needed more training. He went back to Naoum Blinder in San Francisco for a two-year period of hard, intensive work on musical interpretation. Then in 1939 he gave another New York recital. Once again the minuses of critical reaction balanced the pluses. "Transported by his own emotional sincerity," one of the critics wrote, "he might have taken greater heed for tonal balance."

But this same critic found enough promise in Stern's performance to suggest that the name of Isaac Stern was well worth
remembering.

The first significant milestone in Stern's career had been
when he found Naoum Blinder as a teacher. The second came
in 1940, when Alexander Zakin became his accompanist. Zakin
had come to America to further his career as pianist and
teacher. Several lucrative propositions were offered him almost
at once. He was mulling over which one to accept when he
heard Stern play. Without hesitation he decided to forego
his own opportunities for the sake of becoming Stern's accompanist and working with him toward the attainment of a goal
which Zakin knew was inevitable—Stern's greatness. They
worked together day after day, sometimes for ten hours, as
Stern concentrated on repertory and technique.

Then, at a recital in Carnegie Hall on January 12, 1943,
Zakin's faith in Stern was realized. Now the critic of the New
York *Post* called him "a master of his instrument." Virgil
Thomson referred to him in the *Herald Tribune* as "one of the
world's master fiddlers." Louis Biancolli in the *World Tele-
gram and Sun* placed him in the "top rank" of living violinists.

Similar enthusiasm was sounded across the country as Stern
embarked on his first national tour. John Rosenfeld of the
Dallas *Morning News*, one of the most astute critics of the
Southwest, let out all the stops in his enthusiasm by saying that
Stern's technique compared to Heifetz's, Stern's tone to
Elman's, Stern's communicativeness to Kreisler's, and Stern's
dedication to music to Menuhin's. He concluded: "Stern is
one of the greatest contemporary violinists, fully entitled to
a place on the bench of the mighty."

Stern's remarkable artistic growth has been a continuing

process since 1943. He has ripened and mellowed as a musician; he has deepened his intellectual resources; he has sharpened his interpretative insight; he has perfected his technique. He now belongs with the all-time immortals of the violin.

He has been heard in every possible place and through every possible medium: in recitals; as guest artist with practically every important orchestra in the world; at the world's leading festivals from Israel to Edinburgh to Prades. He has won world renown as a chamber-music performer, particularly with the trio which he organized with Leonard Rose, cellist, and Eugene Istomin, pianist. He has appeared over every major radio and television network. He has made voluminous recordings for Columbia, some of which have been best sellers. He has even appeared in the movies. He was first heard in motion pictures on the sound track in 1947, when he dubbed in for John Garfield, appearing in *Humoresque* as a successful concert virtuoso. In 1952 Stern not only played the violin on the sound track but even appeared on the screen: in *Tonight We Sing*, the screen biography of Sol Hurok, the concert impresario who also happens to be Stern's manager. In this motion picture Stern represented a great violinist of the past—Eugène Ysaÿe— whom he has long used as his personal model for emulation.

"In many respects," Harold C. Schonberg wrote in a feature article in *The New York Times Magazine*, "he is the complete violinist—that is, one who has tone, technique, musicianship, and above all the ability to project. . . . His bow arm is a legend." To which Schonberg later added in a review: "He represents the modern school of violin playing at its best, and little can be said about him that has not been said many times before. Surety and precision marked all of his work, cleanly turned phrasing, strong rhythm, and impeccable technique."

Stern's prime concern is ever the music, never the performance itself. Schonberg continues: "When he talks about a concerto he is concerned with musical problems, not technical problems. He will not say that he uses this fingering or that bowing; he will say that he phrases in this or that fashion, and that the phrases mean thus and so."

He likes to practice late at night, until the early hours of dawn—even though he has previously gone through a strenuous day and evening—because the quiet and peace of nighttime he finds most conducive to concentration. He does not usually try to keep in technical trim through scales and exercises the way a good many other violinists do. "When I think I need scales," he has said, "I play scales." But most often he concentrates on repertory and in studying new compositions. "This way I have no predetermined physical approach. My fingers have not become solidified."

His comparative indifference to personal aggrandizement is exemplified by his attitudes toward modern music. He has played as much as, if not more, new violin music than perhaps any other performer of today. But the kudos a performer gets from presenting important world *premières* or from commissioning new works from major composers does not interest him at all. "If I like a work I play it," is the way he puts it simply and directly. And he never commissions works because one never really knows how such a work will turn out, and he will never play a work he doesn't like.

Yet significant first performances are not lacking with Stern. He has given the world *première* of Hindemith's 1939 *Violin Sonata;* of William Schuman's *Second Violin Concerto* in 1950; of Leonard Bernstein's *Serenade for Violin, Strings and Percussion* at the Venice Festival in 1954; of the revised version of

Schuman's concerto in 1956. His performance of Prokofiev's *First Violin Concerto* early in his career (in 1947) was not, to be sure, a *première*, or even a novelty; but it was significant to point to Stern's uncommon dedication to and rare interpretative powers in modern music. "I was ready to concede," said Louis Biancolli in reviewing that performance, "that if there is one violinist inching close to the great Jascha his name is Isaac Stern. Always accompanying this boy's sturdy technique and tone was something that counted even more in the long run—brain power. It shows in every phrase of his playing. For young Stern has never been content with mere brilliance. Showmanship is out of his line, and so is that super-oily style that goes by the name of *schmalz*. Then he always knows how to adjust tone and style to the music in hand, never crossbreeding two styles in the same composition."

Few if any of our present-day concert artists regularly go through the kind of whirlwind schedule adopted by Stern as normal operating procedure. He is a human dynamo, an unleashed typhoon. He does not seem to know the meaning of fatigue, nor is he ever a victim of either nerves or temperament. He seems to thrive on work and more work—and plays even better at the end of a long, arduous, and taxing tour than at the beginning when he was fresh and rested. In a twenty-two-month period between August 1953 and June 1955 he was involved in a nonstop tour that took him not once but twice around the globe. He gave some three hundred concerts in that time. One of his visits to Israel was typical of his perpetual-motion kind of activity. On Monday morning in Tel Aviv he rehearsed three concertos which were performed that same evening; Tuesday morning he played two more concertos at a Pension Fund concert, then rehearsed for a concert the same

VAN CLIBURN

LEON FLEISHER   BYRON JANIS

GARY GRAFFMAN

ISAAC STERN

GLENN GOULD   LEONARD ROSE

Shulkret

EUGENE ISTOMIN   DANIEL BARENBOIM

DAVID OISTRAKH

JAIME LAREDO   MSTISLAV ROSTROPOVICH

RUGGIERO RICCI

PIERRE FOURNIER

SVIATOSLAV RICHTER

EMIL GILELS

SHMUEL ASHKENASI

DAVID BAR-ILLIAN

JULIAN BREAM

ARTHUR WHITTEMORE AND JACK LOWE

ARTHUR GOLD AND ROBERT FIZDALE

evening when he played three more concertos. On Wednesday he repeated the three-concerto performance in Jerusalem. Then for an encore he played a fourth concerto!

In December 1959 he made twelve appearances in four days with the New York Philharmonic. On each day he played a solo concerto (the musically and technically taxing modern Alban Berg Concerto), participated in a performance of a double concerto (Brahms), and performed the solo violin part in one of Bach's orchestral *Brandenburg Concertos* (No. 5). He took all this in stride, as if it were a normal week's work for a violinist. It is not an unusual year in which he gives as many as one hundred and fifty concerts, striding around the world with seven-league boots which defy space and time. "Stern has given performances with a high fever, a sprained wrist, bent over with fatigue," says Schonberg, "but he drives his pudgy body on and boasts that he has not canceled a single concert in his . . . years before the public." There are some summer visits to Israel when he makes between seventeen and twenty appearances within a week or two. He has become such a favorite in that country that he was the artist called upon to inaugurate the new Mann Auditorium in Tel Aviv in September 1957. During one of his world tours he gave nineteen concerts in ten Japanese cities during a two-week period. Returning from that world tour he did not even bother to catch his breath, undertaking an extended American tour after only a few days' interval. The same thing happened after his experiences in the Soviet Union in 1956. Hardly had he returned to the United States in June when he embarked on a six-week tour of eight South American countries. Then, still without bothering for a rest period, he left for a European tour that culminated with performances at the Edinburgh Festival.

At Columbia Records his capacity for work is a legend. "On a typical day," Schonberg reveals, "he will work at the studio from 10 A.M. to 1 P.M., knock off for lunch, go back and work from two to six, go out for a Gargantuan dinner, go back to the studio at eight and make tapes until 1 A.M. Then he will beg for more time: 'Please, please, I'm just getting warmed up.'"

Harness this energy, capacity for work, and drive to a good cause, and the impossible becomes possible. This is what happened a number of years ago. Carnegie Hall, for many years New York's temple of great music and the scene of grandiose music making for more than half a century, seemed doomed. A new concert hall was being erected at Lincoln Center, the Philharmonic Auditorium. A giant financial deal involving millions was set into motion to raze Carnegie Hall to the ground and build a mammoth office building—the property on Fifty-seventh Street and Seventh Avenue being one of the most valuable in the city. To destroy such a historic musical monument seemed to Stern a desecration. He went into action, and accomplished what everybody said couldn't be done. The financial deal was stopped cold. Stern got the city of New York to buy Carnegie Hall instead, and lease it to a nonprofit organization of which he became president. In September 1961 Stern flew in to New York (between engagements in Switzerland and England) to appear for a single performance with the New York Philharmonic to celebrate the saving of Carnegie Hall. He was given a standing ovation by an appreciative public.

Early in his career Stern married and divorced the famous American ballerina, Nora Kaye. In 1951, while performing in Israel, he fell in love with the lovely blond Israeli girl, Vera Lindeblit. Sweeping her off her feet in a ten-day courtship, he

66

married her in November of the same year. They set up home in an apartment in New York City overlooking Central Park, where they are raising their three children, a daughter and two sons.

Like many an American, Stern has always been interested in sports. As a youngster he was a rabid baseball fan, knew the batting and pitching averages of his favorites, the standings of the major-league clubs on any given day, and the daily scores. He has retained some of this interest and can still occasionally be found at the ball park or in front of the television screen when his favorite team, the Yankees, is playing. He used to play an excellent game of tennis and ping-pong. Today he keeps fit mainly by swimming or walking. His favorite diversions include reading books, playing a game of gin rummy (he invariably loses, since he is always taking chances), and perpetrating practical jokes on helpless, unsuspecting friends.

LEONARD ROSE

[1918–   ]

THE TRIO which Isaac Stern had helped to organize and of which he was violinist—and which has now become one of the most distinguished ensembles in the world—includes Leonard Rose, cellist, and Eugene Istomin, pianist.

Leonard Rose and his cello have known not one but three careers in music. The first part of Rose's professional career was devoted to the first-desk cello duties in symphony orchestras: from 1939 to 1943 with the Cleveland Orchestra; from 1943 to 1951 with the New York Philharmonic. The first-desk cellist is required to play solo parts when the symphonic work calls for them—for example, in works such as Brahms's *Second Piano Concerto* or Richard Strauss's tone poem *Don Quixote*. But beyond this the first cellist has the obligation to solve for the cellists behind him whatever unusual technical problems might be found in the music, a by no means infrequent chore where complex modern scores are involved. In short, the first cellist is the one-star general over the cello troops, serving under a five-star general, who is the conductor. The conductor must have confidence in him, must rely completely and implicitly on him in anything and everything that concerns the cello section.

69

As first-desk cellist, Leonard Rose proved himself to be the best in the business. The world-famous conductors under whom he worked for so many years recognized his value. "I consider Leonard Rose one of the outstanding cellists of our time," said George Szell, conductor of the Cleveland Orchestra. Bruno Walter (who often appeared as conductor of the New York Philharmonic) wrote: "Leonard Rose's profound musicianship, technical perfection, his emotional warmth and rare beauty of his tone have been a source of pure joy for me in all the years of our musical association. The cause of the cello's musical literature can be in no better hands than his." And Dimitri Mitropoulos, music director of the New York Philharmonic when Rose was its first cellist, had this to say of him: "I consider Leonard Rose the superlative cellist of today. He is the finest I have ever worked with, possessing all the qualities that make a great artist."

But a cellist in a symphony orchestra—even a first cellist—can hardly be permitted to give full and free expression to his temperament and personality; he must make them subservient to the will and concepts of the conductor. This is the reason that, in 1951, Leonard Rose—feeling the artistic necessity to express himself in music as an individualist—decided to leave the first-desk cello of the New York Philharmonic and thus bring an end to one musical career in favor of another. On April 5, 1951, he made the transition from symphony orchestra first cellist to a virtuoso by appearing as a soloist in two major works with the New York Philharmonic (the Saint-Saëns *A minor Concerto* and Ernest Bloch's rhapsody *Schelomo*). "It was in the nature of a public farewell," explained Howard Taubman, the music critic of *The New York Times.* "The truth, of course, is that Mr. Rose has been a virtuoso of the cello for some time, but his playing has always been a blend of technical musicianship and a simple, innate modesty. He may have to step out a little more in the months ahead, but it is hard to believe that his essential musical personality will change much."

He stepped out in 1951–1952 on an extended tour of the United States. His first circuit of Europe's music centers took place in 1958, highlighted by a brilliant performance at the World's Fair in Brussels. He then went on to perform throughout Latin America, and in August 1961 he paid his first visit to Israel. In 1962–1963, besides appearances from Mexico City to Tel Aviv, he gave four concerts in New York City; was a featured artist at the opening festivities of the Seattle World's Fair; was asked to give a concert at the White House for President and Mrs. John F. Kennedy. In 1962–1963 he was also a stellar attraction in major music festivals from Israel to Edinburgh, Scotland.

On the concert stage, as a virtuoso, Leonard Rose remained what he had been as first-desk man in symphony orchestras: a musician with the instincts, tastes, and understanding of the true artist; a cellist with a tone that sang opulently and retained its purity in all ranges of dynamics; a consummate technique; a commanding personality able to capture the fascinated interest of audiences everywhere; a gift at communication that made him at one with his hearers. What Louis Biancolli once wrote in the New York *World Telegram* was a reflection of the general critical consensus: "My guess is that Leonard Rose is the best cellist since Pablo Casals."

Having thus solidified his place as cello virtuoso in the concert world, Leonard Rose went on to make still a third musical career for himself—as a chamber musician. With two other

71

equally extraordinary musicians—Eugene Istomin, pianist, and Isaac Stern, violinist—he helped to form a trio which made its debut in New York City in 1962 with a performance of Beethoven's *Triple Concerto* with the New York Philharmonic. This new organization was accurately described by Paul Henry Lang in the *Herald Tribune* as a "trio of virtuosos," but virtuosos who stood ready to sublimate their own personalities and artistic idiosyncrasies for the sake of great ensemble playing. The result was, as Lang noted, "an evening of music making without frills when three great musicians play as if for themselves, to their own satisfaction, and we just sat there thankful that such a thing is possible." A series of three trio concerts in New York soon after this led Irving Kolodin of the *Saturday Review* to remark that their achievement was "beyond the reach of any other group of players now performing." Since then the Istomin–Stern–Rose trio has appeared in concerts and music festivals the world over; and wherever it is heard it becomes a red-letter event.

Leonard Rose was born in Washington, D.C., on July 26, 1918. His family moved to Florida while he was still a child. It was there that he began taking cello lessons—with Walter Grossman. When Rose was thirteen he won first prize in the cello division in the Florida State Contest for performing artists. This, in turn, led to several concert appearances in Florida. In his fifteenth year Rose came to New York, where his studies were continued with Frank Miller, first cellist of Arturo Toscanini's NBC Symphony Orchestra. (Miller also happened to be Rose's cousin.) In 1934 a scholarship enabled Rose to complete his cello education with a four-year period of study with Felix Salmond, as distinguished a virtuoso as he was a teacher, at the Curtis Institute in Philadelphia.

Salmond pronounced Rose ready for a professional career in music in 1938. Rose auditioned for Toscanini who forthwith engaged the young man as a cellist for the NBC Symphony. Rose was only three weeks with the orchestra when Toscanini elevated him to the post of assistant first cellist. At the end of the season Rose left the NBC Symphony to become the first cellist of the Cleveland Orchestra. Then only twenty years of age, Rose forthwith became one of the youngest men ever to occupy a first-cello desk with a major American symphony orchestra. While fulfilling his duties as orchestral musician for four years, Rose made fourteen appearances as guest artist with the Cleveland Orchestra, throwing for the first time the limelight on his potential as a virtuoso.

Then in 1943 Rose was summoned back to New York to become the first cellist of the Philharmonic. He filled that post with rare grace and distinction for eight years. The last time he played with the orchestra as one of its members was in 1951 in Edinburgh, Scotland, where the orchestra had gone to participate in its celebrated Scottish music festival.

Besides his concert appearances Rose has made numerous recordings of the major works in cello literature for Columbia Masterworks. One of his recordings—that of the Brahms's *Double Concerto* which he performed with Isaac Stern under the direction of Bruno Walter—received in 1957 the Grand Prix du Disque, the highest award that Europe can confer in recorded music.

On the rare occasions when Rose can call his time his own he spends it at home in Great Neck, Long Island. His wife, Minna—who died in 1964—was once a viola player. She met Rose when both were students at the Curtis Institute. She surrendered all thoughts of a concert career for herself when

73

she married, preferring to devote herself for the next quarter of a century completely to husband and children. At the time of her death both Rose children were fully grown, ready to set off on their own—a daughter, aged twenty-three, and a son, aged twenty.

For diversion Rose used to enjoy playing golf and ping-pong. Today his main recreation lies in stimulating conversations with his friends, in sharing his time with his children, and on special occasions in cooking special dishes for a festive meal.

EUGENE ISTOMIN

[1925–   ]

THE PIANIST of the celebrated chamber-music ensemble comprising Leonard Rose, cellist, Isaac Stern, violinist, and Eugene Istomin, pianist, is an artist who had become a veteran of the concert wars by the time he was forty.

Some performers come to fame by virtue of winning a major international competition. Eugene Istomin first arrived both at world recognition and at full artistic maturity by appearing at a significant international music festival. He was young, unknown, and far from his musical prime when, in 1950, he was invited to participate in the first festival held in Prades, France. This is the festival founded and directed by Pablo Casals to help celebrate the bicentenary of Johann Sebastian Bach's death. Pablo Casals came out of retirement to play his cello again and to remind the world why for a generation he was considered the greatest instrumentalist of them all. But besides his appearance as a virtuoso, Casals also conducted a chamber orchestra, with which Istomin appeared as guest artist. "He is destined for a great career," Casals said of his playing. "He is already among our greatest pianists." After that, with the festival become an annual event either in

Prades, or nearby Perpignan, Casals recalled Istomin to appear regularly with him year after year, either in the presentation of major piano concertos or in performances of chamber music in which Casals participated. "Istomin proved to be a revelation," wrote Howard Taubman from Prades in *The New York Times*. "His piano sang; not once did he forget that he was part of an intimate chamber-music group." Istomin also became a major attraction at the Pablo Casals Festival in San Juan, Puerto Rico, which was inaugurated as an annual event in 1956.

Thus Istomin became (by virtue of Casals's enthusiasm and blessings) a world figure in music. But something even more significant than fame happened to Istomin in Prades and Perpignan. As a result of his intensive musical collaboration with Pablo Casals—and by virtue of his own sensitivity and extraordinary musicianship that could readily and quickly profit from such a valuable association—Istomin developed from a skilful pianist into an aristocratic one. Before 1950 he had demonstrated that he had fluency, assurance, and brilliance. But after 1950 discriminating musicianship, exquisite phrasing, a soaring tone, and an immaculate taste also became part of his keyboard equipment. Both as a virtuoso and as a chamber-music performer Istomin scaled new heights after his appearances with Casals. Here is what Louis Biancolli said in the New York *World Telegram and Sun* after Istomin had spent two festival seasons with Casals: "It was a new Eugene Istomin who sat at the piano last night. It was an Istomin for whom technique has ceased to exist for its own sake; an Istomin who found poetry where he had once been contented with prose. In short, an Istomin who had grown to full stature as an artist." Discussing Istomin's performance of Beethoven's *Fourth*

Piano Concerto in San Francisco in 1954, Alfred Frankenstein wrote in the *Chronicle:* "The impression of the whole was of lyrical perfection, superbly restrained, and eloquent by virtue of its subtly sympathetic utterance rather than by virtue of rhetorical flourish. . . . One has seldom heard the scales and trills of the *Fourth Concerto* sing so meaningfully. But the whole thing sang magnificently, and it ended in a mood of infectious wit and gaiety which, one suspects, was far closer to Beethoven's intentions than the stormy display of virtuosity which is sometimes provided in the finale."

Eugene Istomin was born in New York City on November 26, 1925. His parents had been concert singers who had fled from the Soviet Union to find a new and permanent home in the United States. At four the child Istomin was improvising tunes at the piano. At six he served as accompanist to his mother, then appearing in a song recital at the Academy of Music in Brooklyn. Alexander Siloti—former pupil of Liszt and Tchaikovsky, and one of the most venerated pianists and piano teachers of his generation—was in the audience at the Brooklyn Academy. He went backstage to tell Eugene's mother how highly he esteemed the child's talent, and to urge her to forego any further public appearances for him for the sake of serious music study. Kariena, Siloti's daughter, was recruited to give the child his preliminary instruction. After that he was enrolled at the Mannes School of Music in New York City, where his teachers included Ralph Wolfe and Sascha Gorodnitsky at the piano, and Constanin Svedoff in harmony and theory.

Although the music in general, and the piano in particular, now became the core of the boy's life, they did not exclude other interests and pursuits. For one thing he was a passionate

77

baseball fan, and like many another American boy he spent a good deal of his time on sand lots. For another, his parents had insisted that he receive a thorough academic education. Beginning with his tenth year each weekday, up to two in the afternoon, was devoted to the Professional Children's School in Manhattan.

In 1939 he was graduated from the Professional Children's School. He now enrolled at the Curtis Institute in Philadelphia for several years of intensive piano training with Mieczyslaw Horszowski and Rudolf Serkin. All this time public appearances had been scrupulously avoided. But then came the time to test his mettle. In 1943 he entered the Youth Contest sponsored by the Philadelphia Orchestra. He won first prize. This encouraged him to enter the even more important competition, the Leventritt Award, the same year. Here, too, he came through with banners flying. By virtue of the Leventritt Award, he made his official debut in November of 1943 as a soloist of the Philadelphia Orchestra, Eugene Ormandy conducting, in a performance of Chopin's *F minor Concerto*. This was immediately followed by an appearance with the New York Philharmonic under Artur Rodzinski in Brahms's *B-flat major Concerto*. The critics sang his praises. The following season the New York Philharmonic invited him to return and he appeared as soloist with the Little Symphony Society, conducted by Adolf Busch, both in New York and on tour. But all this was just the prelude to his appearance at the Casals Festival in Prades in 1950, followed immediately by his first European tour that included performances in recitals and with orchestra in Italy, Switzerland, and France.

His first tours of South America and South Africa came in 1955, followed in 1956 by his first appearances in Iceland,

Australia, and the Far East. By 1962 (when he took a year's sabbatical from concert work in order to re-evaluate himself and his art and to gain a new and fresh perspective) he had concertized in six continents, in places as widely separated as Iceland and Israel, Saigon and Hong Kong. He has been heard and acclaimed in the world's great festivals, not only in those directed by Casals in Puerto Rico and at Prades, but also at Menton in southern France, at Edinburgh, in Israel, at Athens and Tanglewood; he was also one of the principal artists at the World's Fair in Seattle. He made distinguished recordings for Columbia of his festival performances at Prades in 1950 and 1952 and at Perpignan in 1951, as well as of major concertos by Bach, Rachmaninoff, Beethoven, and Tchaikovsky (the last three with the Philadelphia Orchestra conducted by Ormandy).

Discussing his individual approach to the art of musical interpretation, Istomin has explained: "It is a matter of having something to say in your own way. Such indications as rests and stops, fortes and pianissimos, are helps but do not paint a complete picture. The coloring and the rest is up to me. Instinctively, as well as intellectually, I attempt to work out an interpretation that seems for me sort of inevitable. Then I feel that I am close to the way Beethoven must have wished it to be performed. If I manage to convince an audience of the validity of my approach, then I know that I have had a successful concert."

Since he is a bachelor, Istomin is able to devote whatever time he can snatch from his numerous concert and recording commitments to his extramusical passions: modern art and archaeology, and ancient history. He became fascinated with art following his first visit to France. Today, besides visiting galleries the world over, Istomin has become a collector in his own right. His prize art works include an original Paul Klee (which he bought for only $500 but which is now worth almost ten times that amount), an original Picasso acquired in 1959, and the work of Renoir and several other Impressionists. Istomin's art possessions also include statues and masks several thousand years old, and a priceless blue Persian plate which an artist presented him after one of his concerts in Teheran.

After Istomin's first visit to Greece in 1954 he became absorbed in both ancient history and archaeology. He has since not only read omniverously in both areas, but has also done research and explorations on his own, with the result that he has become something of an authority in both fields.

RUGGIERO RICCI

[1920–   ]

JAIME LAREDO

[1941–   ]

A GOOD MANY of today's world-famous concert artists were
once child prodigies. But the number of prodigies who grow
up to maturity as world-famous artists are few and far between. Year after year bright-faced, eager, and highly talented
children come before audiences with a technique and a presentation of musical literature to inspire incredulity and awe.
These children often gather formidable successes; they become
the cynosure for musical audiences everywhere; they inspire
the most lavish praises; they offer the richest possible hopes
for their future. But only a few become the elect to realize
these hopes. Sometimes success and financial rewards have
come too quickly, softening the prodigy toward that kind of
hard work that is always essential for the cultivation of even
the greatest talent into full flower. Sometimes, while growing
up, these prodigies fail to mature properly as musicians or as

human beings. Sometimes these prodigies fail to develop further as virtuosos for the simple reason that they had already gone as far in their art as they are capable, they have already exhausted their artistic potential.

Ruggiero Ricci, a violinist, was, however, able to outgrow all the successes, temptations, and problems that a phenomenal success as prodigy brought him, to become a mature artist the world admires and respects. The musical gifts with which he was born, and which he revealed from infancy on, were truly extraordinary.

He was born on July 24, 1920, in San Francisco to a humble Italian family. His father had been a day laborer who, when Ricci came into the world, served in uniform as a bandmaster at the army base in San Francisco. The father played and taught the trombone, and was adept at the violin. One day, after little Ruggiero heard his father perform one of Brahms's *Hungarian Dances,* he decided he, too, wanted to become a violinist. He asked his father for lessons and began getting them after he had been presented with a miniature violin.

The remarkable way in which the child Ricci absorbed whatever was taught him convinced the father that an experienced teacher was called for. One of the best in San Francisco was Louis Persinger, who two years earlier had been in the news when one of his prodigies, the child Yehudi Menuhin, gave a sensational concert. It was to Louis Persinger that father Ricci turned to for advice and guidance. Persinger stood ready to assume the responsibility of Ricci's development, placing him for preliminary instruction under one of his assistants, Mary Elizabeth Lackey. It did not take her long to become aware of the child's phenomenal gifts. She soon decided to devote herself completely to his proper artistic growth. In order that the child might live with her, and thus be under her continual supervision, she legally became the boy's guardian in November 1928.

The year 1928 was the one in which Ricci made his formal debut. This took place in San Francisco in a performance of the Mendelssohn *Violin Concerto* which local critics described as "fantastic." A year later—on October 20, 1929—he repeated this performance in New York City, this time as soloist of the Manhattan Symphony directed by Henry Hadley. "Master Ricci," wrote Samuel Chotzinoff, the distinguished music critic of the New York *World*, who had formerly been Jascha Heifetz's accompanist for a number of years, "revealed a technical mastery of the violin and a genius for interpretation which place him in a class with a handful of the great violinists." Olin Downes reported in *The New York Times* that Ricci was "a born virtuoso and more a true *Wunderkind;* all that great violinists do, he did."

When Ricci returned to New York City for a recital one year later his admirers and friends who packed Carnegie Hall to capacity showered him with bravos and applause. But remembering that, after all, he was still a child of nine, they also filled the artist's room backstage with toys of every description.

An ugly episode now temporarily interfered with the blossoming of a career begun so promisingly. Eager to regain the custody of their son, the elder Riccis went to court. A bitter and prolonged legal struggle ensued that received a good deal of publicity in the newspapers, and particularly in sensation-seeking tabloids. Charges were leveled against Ricci's parents, teacher, and manager for exploiting a child for selfish ends. Finally Mayor James J. Walker was compelled to cancel a projected Carnegie Hall recital by Ricci (which once again was completely sold out) while awaiting a decision from a justice of the New York State Supreme Court on Ricci's exact status as a child performer.

Enmeshed in problems that were far beyond his comprehension, and caught in a fierce tug of war between teacher and parents to both of whom he was devoted, Ricci suffered severely, and his playing reacted accordingly. Then on his own he deserted his teacher to return to his parents; and in time the courts decided in favor of this move. It took awhile for the boy's life to revert to normalcy. When it finally did, his former prodigious powers at the violin returned. He was now able to resume his concert career.

In 1932, when only twelve, he toured Europe. His performances in Berlin, Vienna, London, and Paris were hailed by audiences, critics, and some of Europe's leading cultural and political personalities. At a Berlin recital Ricci was effusively congratulated by the world's foremost scientist, Albert Einstein; by Chancellor von Papen; by Germany's foremost dramatist, Gerhart Hauptmann.

Ricci returned to the American concert scene for the first time since the resolution of his court action with a recital at Carnegie Hall on November 24, 1934. This appearance was described as a "comeback"—a comeback, mind you, by somebody who was only fourteen years old! "He has now the stature of a young violinist of parts, brilliantly gifted, and a sincere musician," reported Olin Downes. Concerts all over the United States followed, together with a second tour of Europe in 1938.

World War II was the hiatus that separated Ricci the prodigy from Ricci the artist. In 1942 he enlisted in the Army

Air Force. Assigned to Special Service, he served for three years by playing the violin in hospitals and camps. These years of concertizing for his fellow G.I.'s proved to be significant for Ricci's development and growth as a concert performer. Since he could not procure a suitable accompanist for many of his appearances, Ricci had to rely more and more on the literature for unaccompanied violin. Years later, after he had returned to the professional concert stage, he was to make a unique place for himself among the violinists of the day with programs devoted exclusively to unaccompanied violin music —and most especially to the *Twenty-Four Caprices* of Paganini of which he became a supreme interpreter.

After the war Ricci was no longer the sweet, round-faced, innocent child appealing to audiences through his precociousness and through the pretty picture he presented on the concert stage. He was now a man—short, squat, somewhat awkward in manner. His was basically not the kind of personality that fascinates and magnetizes an audience on first contact; he had nothing of the matinee idol about him. His appeal had to rest exclusively on the music he played and on the way he played it. But that proved enough.

His return to the concert world came in November 1946 with a Carnegie Hall recital devoted entirely to unaccompanied violin compositions. Once again the critics hailed him. One of them said that his playing was "exemplary of the finest, most sensitive, and most beautiful manipulation of the violin you may expect to hear anywhere." When, six years later, he paid his first return visit to London since 1932, he once again gave a program of unaccompanied music—this time against the advice of a manager who felt such a program would prove a bore. The audience, however, was enchanted.

85

The critics raved. Ricci was instantly contracted to make six more appearances in London.

Today Ricci makes more than a hundred appearances in concert auditoriums from Hong Kong to Helsinki and from New York to Buenos Aires. These performances—combined with the library of violin music he has recorded for London and Decca—have lifted him to a top rank among present-day violinists. The full range of his remarkable versatility and the infinite variety of his style were proved in New York City in the winter of 1964 when he undertook one of the most ambitious assignments ever assumed by a concert violinist. He performed all the major violin concertos in a series of four concerts with orchestra—twelve masterworks in all, from Bach to Hindemith and Prokofiev.

Ricci makes his home in Geneva, Switzerland, with his two daughters and their mother, the former Valma Rodriguez, an Argentine actress. This is his second marriage. The first had taken place during the war, and had been to a young violinist who had studied with Persinger. Ricci had three children by this first marriage.

In an article for *Musical America* James Lyons has emphasized how completely Ricci has made the transition from prodigy to artist. "Because he is a diminutive person he inclines to certain swagger," says Lyons, "but this hint of flamboyance is belied altogether in his friendly, disarming manner. And no one could spend an evening with his family without knowing that it is one of the happiest in the business."

Jaime Laredo stands apart from most other young violinists of today on several counts. A Bolivian by birth—but an American by training and education—he is the only South American ever to win a major international competition. In 1959 he captured first prize in the world-famous Queen Elizabeth Competition for violinists in Brussels. He is the only South American violinist ever to achieve world renown. And, as a cultural attaché to the Bolivian Mission, he was the youngest member in the United Nations. He has also served as the United States representative in Europe under the auspices of the *Jeunesses musicales*—this at the personal request of the then first lady, Mrs. John F. Kennedy. His dazzling virtuosity, his fiery temperament, his sensitive musicianship helped win for America (North as well as South) many new friends abroad. In addition to all these achievements, Jaime Laredo has been designated as "the best young performing artist of the year" by the Institute of the Recording Arts and Sciences for his first RCA-Victor record-album release, "Presenting Jaime Laredo."

Young though he is, Jaime Laredo has already acquired an enviable following both on this continent and abroad. As Howard Taubman said of him in *The New York Times* when Laredo first played in New York: "He has all the technical skills a fine fiddler needs: a sure left hand, a sensitive, supple bow arm, and a tone of color and plasticity." His virtuosity is dazzling. But virtuosity is never exploited for its own sake. Behind the pyrotechnics lies an artistry capable of encompassing the entire literature of the violin with as much musicianly grace and penetration as with technical facility. Perhaps the highest tribute that any violinist can command is the praise of other violinists. Some of Jaime Laredo's fans are to be found among his rivals, many more famous than he. Mischa Elman spoke rhapsodically of his "extraordinary talent" while Zino Francescatti called him "one of the greatest talents I

87

have heard in years." Musicians in other fields have also given voice to their high regard—George Szell, for example, the distinguished conductor of the Cleveland Orchestra. "I consider him," said Szell, "one of the great hopes among young violinists."

Although too young to have much of a past, and young enough to have most of his career still in front of him, Jaime Laredo already is a valuable asset to the concert scene. He belongs rightfully to those aristocratic ranks that produced a Fritz Kreisler, a Jascha Heifetz, a Nathan Milstein, a Zino Francescatti, a Mischa Elman, and an Isaac Stern. Among the younger generation of concert violinists few seem more likely to carry on their noble traditions than he.

Born in Cochabamba, Bolivia, on June 8, 1941, Jaime Laredo was raised from babyhood in a musical atmosphere. His parents were devoted music lovers who often entertained professional musicians as guests. They gave informal concerts for the Laredos and their friends, which the child Jaime listened to with rapt fascination. The local string quartet also used to rehearse at the Laredo home. It was not long before Jaime, aged five, graduated from the ranks of listener to page turner—for already he could read music with facility.

His music study began with Solfeggio. When he was six he received the gift of a violin. Instinctively he tuned it to concert pitch without the help of either a piano or a pitch pipe. For two years Jaime studied locally with Carlo Flamini. Becoming fully aware of the child's extraordinary gifts, Flamini persuaded Laredo's parents to bring him to the United States so that he might profit from the kind of instruction which he deserved and which was not available in Bolivia.

Aged seven, Jaime was brought by his family to San Francisco. There he was enrolled for academic study at the Laurel Village School. At the same time he studied the violin first with Antonio de Grassi, then with Frank Houser. During this period he gave several public demonstrations of his musical gifts. When he was eight he gave a recital in Sacramento, California—an ambitious program that included the Mendelssohn *Concerto*. Three years after that Arthur Fiedler—the well-known conductor of the Boston "Pops" concerts—invited him to be a guest soloist with the San Francisco Symphony, which Fiedler had been invited to direct for a special performance.

In 1953 the Laredos moved to Cleveland. Academic studies were now undertaken with private tutors, and the violin with Josef Gingold, concertmaster of the Cleveland Orchestra. Concert appearances continued to point up his development. In 1955 he gave recitals in Cleveland and Washington, D.C.; and in 1956 he made a concert tour of Peru, Bolivia, and Puerto Rico.

Laredo's violin training was completed in Philadelphia with Ivan Galamian at the Curtis Institute. His academic studies were ended at the Lincoln Preparatory School in the same city. While still Galamian's pupil, Laredo gave a recital in Washington, D.C., on January 8, 1959 (under the auspices of the Pan American Union), in which he revealed himself the fully-developed artist. Paul Hume said in the Washington *Post:* "He is going to be one of the great names in violin playing." It was on the strength of this performance that Arthur Judson placed Laredo under the Columbia Artists Management for extended concert tours.

Laredo was graduated from the Curtis Institute in May 1959. Hardly was the diploma in hand when he left for

Brussels to enter the Queen Elizabeth Competition. Winning the first prize in violin (the first South American ever to do so in any category) made him something of a national hero in Bolivia. The country showered him with honors and tributes of every description when he returned to his native land soon after receiving the award. He was a public idol. The grateful country even issued twelve stamps with his picture. This is one of the rare instances, incidentally, where a living musician (creative or interpretative) has thus been honored; and surely never before did it come to one only twenty-two years old.

Since that time Laredo has toured Europe and the United States several times, besides making distinguished recordings for RCA-Victor. In 1960 he married Ruth Meckler, a young pianist who had also studied at the Curtis Institute. On several occasions Ruth has served as his accompanist, but her major preoccupation now is to cater to the needs, comforts, and well-being of a husband whose ascent to the topmost rungs of his profession seems a foregone conclusion.

PIERRE FOURNIER

[1906-   ]

SINCE THE END of World War II France has contributed a cellist of extraordinary attainments to the concert scene. He is Pierre Fournier. Recognizing his lofty place in French concert music, a grateful government made him Chevalier of the Legion of Honor in 1953 and, a decade later, elevated him to the rank of Officier. Renowned French writers, in dedicating some of their works to him, have spoken of him with ringing phrases. Colette, for example, said of Fournier's cello that it "sings better than anything else sings." André Gide recalled "vivid memories of unforgettable musical moments." French newspapers have at different times described him as an "aristocrat of musicians," a "sorcerer of the cello," and a "poet and prince of the cello."

It took a calamity to make Pierre Fournier into a cellist in the first place. He was born in Paris on June 24, 1906, to a distinguished family. His grandfather had been a famous sculptor—a designer of some of Paris's notable monuments including the Pont Alexandre III that spans the Seine River. Pierre's father derived his fame from military and political accomplishments, having served as a general of the French

91

army during World War I and later holding the post of governor in Corsica.

Pierre's father hoped the boy would follow in his footsteps. But the mother, an excellent amateur pianist, had ideas of her own. These ideas prevailed because the father also loved good music. When the mother discovered how soundly musical were Pierre's instincts, she decided to do everything she could to develop them. She gave him piano lessons. Then, seeing how remarkable his progress was, she became fired with the ambition to make him a concert pianist.

It was then that tragedy struck and changed the direction Pierre would henceforth travel in music. When he was nine he was stricken by infantile paralysis. For a while it seemed that never again would he have the use of his limbs. But a miraculous recovery followed that promised him a normal, healthy life. However, the movement of his legs had been slightly impaired, making it difficult for him to negotiate the piano pedals. Compelled to abandon the study of the piano, Pierre—encouraged by his parents—turned to the cello, an instrument that had always fascinated him. "The idea of trying to *sing* with a stringed instrument," he now explains, "captured my imagination."

When he was thirteen Pierre entered the Paris Conservatory. There, during the next few years, he studied with Lucien Capet and Jean Gallon. After graduating from the Conservatory with highest honors in cello, Fournier completed his study of the cello with André Hekking, one of France's most eminent cello virtuosos and teachers.

For a while, following the conclusion of his studies, Fournier played in various orchestras and chamber-music ensembles in Paris. Then, when he was nineteen, he turned to the concert platform. His debut came about when he was invited to appear as soloist with the Colonne Orchestra in Paris. This performance proved so successful that he immediately was asked to play with other major European symphonic groups. Recitals now added further to his growing reputation. By 1939 he had become such a favorite in Germany that he was required that year to give thirty-two concerts in Berlin alone to meet the demand of his audiences. Meanwhile, Fournier had also embarked upon a highly successful career as a teacher of the cello. From 1937 to 1939 he was professor of cello and chamber music at the École Normale de Musique in Paris. Later on (from 1941 to 1949) he was professor of cello at the Paris Conservatory.

The years of World War II, of course, brought his concert and teaching activities to a temporary halt. But once the war ended, Fournier could resume where he had left off. He now expanded his concert work to global dimensions. In 1945 he made his debut in England as a soloist with the London Philharmonic. "The quiet beauty of his playing," said the critic of the London *Times*, "seemed to create a timeless moment in which again the happy daydream of man could communicate its happiness to its auditors." In 1947 he scored a triumph in appearances with orchestra at the Edinburgh Festival in Scotland. (He has since that time returned to this festival frequently and has become one of its stellar attractions.) Then in 1948 he paid his first visit to the United States—his debut at Town Hall, New York City, serving as a prelude to coast-to-coast appearances. The critics throughout the country showered him with accolades. "Pierre Fournier," said Cyrus Durgin in the Boston *Globe*, "is a very great cellist and an exceptional musician. . . . Technical virtuosity, mastery of style are all blended and directed toward making music. The tone is satiny. The phrasing has utmost grace. Such is the combined mastery and superior perception of this artist that everything was set forth with equal excellence." In the *New York Herald Tribune* Virgil Thomson wrote: "I do not know his superior among living cellists, nor any . . . who give one more profoundly the feeling of having been present at music making of the highest order." Harriet Johnson called him in the New York *Post* "the Keats of his instrument."

His first South American tour, in 1949, supplemented by tours of the Far East, South Africa, and the Soviet Union, extended the sphere of his concert activity and his fame to the farthest reaches. Today Fournier averages about a hundred appearances a year, and his itinerary circles the globe. In 1962–1963, for example, he made his fourth tour of South America and South Africa; his second tour of Japan and the Far East; his ninth tour of the United States. He is a frequent visitor to some of the world's most highly esteemed music festivals, including those at Salzburg, Lucerne, and Edinburgh. He is also one of the most distinguished recording artists of our time. He can be heard on disks in all of Beethoven's major works for the cello, the six Bach solo suites for cello, and virtually every important cello concerto. On three occasions (1955, 1962, and 1963) he has received the highest award a recording artist can gain, that of the Grand Prix du Disque in Paris. In addition, in 1961, the National Academy of Recording Arts and Sciences awarded him a "Grammy" for his Columbia Masterworks release of Richard Strauss's *Don Quixote*, in which he was a soloist with the Cleveland Orchestra under George Szell.

His enormous repertory extends not only through the literature of the baroque, classical, and romantic periods, but also into the modern school. Contemporary composers of every inclination and style find him to be an ideal interpreter of their cello music. Francis Poulenc, Bohuslav Martinu, and Albert Roussel are some of the composers who have written large cello works for him. Fournier gave all these compositions their world *première*. He has also performed the larger cello works of such twentieth-century composers as Paul Hindemith, Darius Milhaud, Ernest Bloch, and Virgil Thomson. In fact, Fournier's interest in modern music is expansive enough to take in the *avant-garde* composers and American jazz—although where jazz is concerned he is only a listener and not a performer.

Home for the Fourniers is a rambling, tastefully furnished house in Geneva, Switzerland. Fournier's wife is an excellent musician in her own right—a gifted pianist, though not a professional one. However, their son, Jean Fonda, is beginning to achieve recognition as a concert pianist.

Since Pierre Fournier is a chronic collector—and always comes home from his travels with valises full of all kinds of curios—his house is crammed with paintings, *objets d'art*, period pieces of furniture, and interesting odds and ends. Fournier's passion for collecting also includes old coins. Among his other interests are reading literature voraciously (in English and German as well as French), playing tennis, indulging in a social game of cards with friends, visiting museums, and going to the movies.

EMIL GILELS

[1916–   ]

In 1921 SERGE PROKOFIEV, the world-famous Russian composer and pianist, toured the United States. This was the last time in more than thirty years that a Soviet musician would be allowed to appear in America. Then in 1955, in Geneva, an agreement was reached at the summit between President Eisenhower and Premier Khrushchev to encourage a cultural exchange between the United States and the Soviet Union. A free intercourse between these two musical countries was thus suddenly resumed after a lapse of thirty-four years.

The first outstanding performing artist to come to the United States from the Soviet Union under the provisions of this agreement was the pianist Emil Gilels in 1955. He was affectionately dubbed "the little giant" by some of his colleagues: "little," because he was short and stocky; "giant," because of his formidable technical powers. His virtuosity, his digital control, his spellbinding magnetism were said to have found few parallels among concert pianists of the post-World War II era. Gilels could make the piano erupt into a typhoon, and then he could soothe it into a beatific calm. With his strong and steel-like fingers he could shout, but he could also sing.

The music he played, as one critic described it so pictur-
esquely, was "a huge, dark, turbulent flood pouring from his
heart."

Gilels arrived in the United States as 1955 was drawing to a
close. On December 3 he made his American debut in Philadelphia, appearing as a soloist in the Tchaikovsky *First Piano
Concerto* with the Philadelphia Orchestra under Eugene Ormandy. One day later he played the same work in New York
City. The Philadelphia *Inquirer* reported that Gilels's debut
was "the most triumphant . . . played in the Academy of
Music in many decades." The New York *World Telegram
and Sun* described how the audience in Carnegie Hall was "on
its feet cheering wildly when the short, bushy-haired virtuoso
rose from the piano and bowed gravely. It was one of the most
clamorous ovations I have ever heard—and one of the most
deserved."

As for Gilels's performance of the Tchaikovsky *Concerto*
the critics did not seem able to summon enough superlatives to
describe it. "Gilels has everything that it takes to be a top-
grade pianist," said Howard Taubman in *The New York
Times.* "His tone is as solid as his physique with its peasant
sturdiness. His fingers have boundless agility and control. . . .
Best of all, he is a musician of personality. . . . He gave the
work the kind of rousing interpretation possible only to pianists
of his caliber, of whom there are precious few."

Since that first unforgettable impression Gilels has been
frequently heard in the United States, and in a wide and varied
repertory. Though poetic calm and profound reflection are
certainly not lacking in his playing, Gilels is perhaps at his
greatest—perhaps even incomparable today—in works of a
grand design requiring a large tone, rich and swelling dy-

namics, clamorous sounds, and lightning rapidity of fingers. He is of the Russian tradition that had produced Anton Rubinstein in the nineteenth century and Vladimir Horowitz in our own. Just as he does not caress a musical phrase but attacks it, so he does not woo an audience but overwhelms it. He is dramatic rather than lyrical. "He gets into the keys," said Harold C. Schonberg in *The New York Times*, "in a manner reminiscent of the romantic pianists who flourished in the last generation." This is the grand style of piano playing, born with Franz Liszt, a style which was believed to have passed away permanently in our own times. It has been reborn with Emil Gilels.

Gilels was born in Odessa, on the Black Sea, on October 19, 1916. Though neither of his parents was a professional musician, there were much singing and piano playing at the Gilels home. Both his father (by profession a bookkeeper) and his mother were dedicated music lovers, and proficient in playing the piano. While Gilels insists he was no prodigy, he early proved both in public and in private that where music was concerned he was something special. When he was six, he began studing the piano with Jacob Tkach; at nine he gave a private concert; at thirteen he appeared in an impressive public recital.

In 1929 he became a pupil of Bertha Ringold who, he has since said, was the one most responsible for his development. He had been studying with her for about three years when Artur Rubinstein, the world-famous piano virtuoso, visited Odessa. "I was asked by a piano teacher at the local Conservatory to hear her pupils," Rubinstein recalled to an interviewer many years later. "You know how boring such an ordeal usually is, but by God there was a boy—I remember as if it happened yesterday—short, with a mass of red hair and freckles,

99

who played . . . I can't describe it. . . . All I can say is—if he ever comes here I might as well pack up by bags and go."

So impressed was Rubinstein that he advised young Gilels to do something which he had opposed all his life—namely, having a fifteen-year-old boy give up music study and begin concertizing. "There isn't anything more you can learn," Rubinstein told him. But Soviet law forbade the exploitation of minors, and Gilels himself was bent on going through additional training. Between 1932 and 1935 he attended the Odessa Conservatory, a period in which he won first prize in the All Union Musicians Competition for pianists held in Moscow in 1933. In 1935 he enrolled in the Moscow Conservatory, in the master classes of Professor Neuhaus. Gilels did not stay long at that conservatory as a pupil. After gaining second prize in an international piano competition in Vienna in 1936, he graduated from student to teacher by becoming Professor Neuhaus's assistant at the Moscow Conservatory. And after that he captured the first prize in the Queen Elizabeth Competition for pianists in Brussels. In 1938 he initiated his career as concert virtuoso with performances throughout the Soviet Union.

How highly his country regarded him, even at the dawn of his career, can be measured by the fact that (together with the violinist, David Oistrakh) he was selected to visit the United States in 1939 to perform at the Soviet pavilion at the New York World's Fair. The rapidly changing political scene at that time—Soviet *rapprochement* with Nazi Germany followed by the outbreak of World War II—frustrated these plans. Both Gilels and Oistrakh were kept home. Gilels continued giving concerts in the Soviet Union and teaching the piano at the Moscow Conservatory. When the Soviet Union was attacked, Gilels concertized at the front for Soviet soldiers, and in occupied cities. In recognition of his contribution to the war effort, and of his rapidly expanding powers as a virtuoso, Gilels was given in 1946 the highest award the Soviets could bestow on an artist—the Stalin Prize of one hundred thousand rubles. His country continued to shower him with honors. In later years it honored him with the Order of the Red Banner of Labor, the Order of the Sign of Honor, and, most important of all, conferred on him the title of People's Artist of the USSR.

Gilels's first appearance outside the Soviet Union took place at the Third International Spring Festival in Prague in 1948 where he scored a success of the first magnitude. Before he had completed the first part of his program there "it was obvious that we were in the presence of an extraordinary musical talent with supreme powers at his command," as Victor I. Seroff later recalled. In 1951 Gilels was one of eleven Soviet artists sent to participate at the May Music Festival in Florence, Italy. In 1952 he toured Scandinavia, and in 1954 he performed at the Berlin embassy during the Berlin Conference of Foreign Ministers. So frequent and so extensive have Gilels's appearances been outside the Soviet Union—and so enthusiastic has been the reception wherever he has played—that he has been widely (though unofficially) recognized as the Soviet "Ambassador of music"—an ambassador of good music, a representative of Soviet musical culture.

Gilels is about five feet six inches tall, built solidly and compactly. He has a cherubic face topped by a mass of chestnut-colored hair; the intensity of his expression is softened by the gentleness of his eyes. He married a fellow student of the Moscow Conservatory in 1947—a young, petite, and highly gifted pianist who had come from the Georgia region of the Soviet Union. Since her marriage, music has been relegated to a background. Her main interests—outside of her husband's career and raising a daughter—include sculpting. "She is," Gilels told Victor I. Seroff, "my judge and my only counselor." However, so overwrought and upset does she become whenever her husband performs that she refuses to attend his performances; she will even avoid listening to him while he is broadcasting.

When Gilels is not touring the world, he devotes himself in Moscow to making recordings and to his teaching duties as full professor at the Conservatory. He accepts only a scattered handful of students at a time—four or five—and these he teaches privately; he also has two classes a week in piano technique. He maintains that he is a man without any hobbies, never having had the time to develop them. His only escape from music comes from joining family and friends in quiet social evenings at home, which usually end up in more music making and in listening to recordings. His sister is a talented violinist, but not so famous as her husband—Leonid Kogan—who is one of the foremost Soviet violinists of our time.

SVIATOSLAV RICHTER

[1914–   ]

WITH THE FLOODGATES sufficiently lowered after 1954 to allow a flow of distinguished musicians from the Soviet Union to the United States, America was finally enabled to hear for itself some of the artists it had so long known through reputation and recordings. One of them was Sviatoslav Richter.

For a number of years Americans had been told (often by other distinguished concert pianists) that in Richter the world boasted a pianist who was in a class by himself. This statement was not easily accepted by audiences grown up on Serge Rachmaninoff, Vladimir Horowitz, Walter Gieseking, Artur Rubinstein, and Rudolf Serkin. Despite some highly remarkable Richter recordings imported from the Soviet Union, Americans were skeptical that Richter was as good as so many rated him. But as more and more Americans had an opportunity to penetrate the Iron Curtain and hear Richter in person, the laudatory opinions kept coming—and kept mounting in superlatives. Howard Taubman, then the music critic of *The New York Times,* visited Moscow in the spring of 1958 when he heard Richter play the Mozart *D minor Piano Concerto.* He reported back to his newspaper: "To put it simply, he is a superb pianist. . . . His tone is pure velvet. . . . His sense of rhythm is wholly admirable—flexible within a classic framework. His phrasing is sensitive. There is a wealth of nuance, all bent to the demands of the music. This was a radiant, searching reading of Mozart's familiar score."

Thus the appetite of the American music lover for Richter was further whetted. But it was not to be satisfied for another year and a half. Then, in the fall of 1960, Richter made his first tour of the United States—and Americans could finally judge for themselves. His first performance in America, indeed his first performance anywhere outside the Iron Curtain, took place in Chicago on October 15, 1960, when he appeared with the Chicago Orchestra. Five New York recitals followed, at one of which Richter offered five Beethoven sonatas.

Richter now proved why he had become a legend. Here was virtuosity *in excelsis*—but not in the grand bravura style of Emil Gilels. Others might seek out the grand design, be partial to large percussive sounds, enjoy dramatic effects. Richter was continually concerned exclusively with poetic content, was always concentrating on subtle details and nuances, ever striving for and achieving clarity of texture and precision of tempo and rhythm. Temperament, emotion, musicianship were all fused into a single component. Accurate, indeed, was the comment of the Soviet critic, V. Delson, when he said in *Soviet Music:* "Richter's thoroughly emotional virtuosity recognizes no compromises for the sake of technical convenience. . . . When Richter's bold probing into the heart of the music, his temperament, enthusiasm, and imagination are organically united with profound concentration on design, treatment, and conception, his art acquires a tremendous sweep and authority. At such times the power of Richter's playing is limitless."

Richter's personality does not light up an auditorium the way in which Van Cliburn's does. Richter is a slight and undemonstrative man, completely unassuming and self-effacing on the platform. He seems determined to focus the attention and interest of the audience exclusively on the music he is playing. "I don't consider the public," he once told an interviewer with brutal frankness. "My whole interest is my approaching encounter with the composer—and his music." His Slavic, peasant-like face, under a crop of red hair, is so intense as to be almost austere. It is impossible to think of that face giving off a smile—and indeed one never finds him smiling during a performance. His gestures are subdued. Any suggestion of flamboyance or of fiery temperament is scrupulously avoided. Only the inmost meaning of the music becomes the central interest, and Richter seeks out that meaning with a profundity and a penetration not frequently encountered.

One becomes thunderstruck to discover that an adequate training at the piano came to Richter comparatively late in life. He has such a supreme command of the keyboard; his artistic depth and perspective are so unique; his repertory is so immense (it is said he has fifty programs at his fingertips) and demands such versatility, that one naturally assumes that the piano has been his *alter ego* from earliest childhood on.

He was born in the little Ukrainian town of Gitomir, near Kiev, on March 20, 1914. His father (of German extraction) was a trained pianist. While Sviatoslav was still an infant his family moved to Odessa where the father became a member of the Odessa Conservatory faculty. There the boy was given his first piano lessons. Although he demonstrated a passion for music (he transcribed for the piano a whole library of musical masterpieces just for the fun of it) he had no ambition at the time to become a virtuoso. The piano instruction was haphazard, and he was given no lessons in musical theory. What he knew about music he picked up mostly by himself, as best he could, and wherever he could manage to find this information. But he was able to make enough progress in music in his boyhood to become first a pianist and later on when only fifteen years old, a conductor of the Odessa Opera and Ballet Theatre.

Though virtually self-taught even by the time he was nineteen, he gave his first piano recital in a program made up exclusively of Chopin's music. He also did a bit of composing. Then, suddenly feeling the need for more study, he entered the Moscow Conservatory in 1937 where he became a pupil of Heinrich Neuhaus. "Professor Neuhaus," he has since said, "freed my hands—really liberated me. For that reason he is more than a teacher or a friend to me." Richter continually amazed his teacher with his fantastic musical memory and with his altogether incomparable gift to adapt himself to practically every known style and period in music. Three years more and Richter made a public appearance in Moscow when he created a sensation by playing Serge Prokofiev's *Sixth Piano Sonata*. Prokofiev jumped from his seat in the audience, rushed to the stage, and planted a kiss on Richter's cheek. Since that time Richter has become probably the most significant interpreter of Prokofiev's piano music; some of that composer's greatest works for piano were dedicated to him.

Despite this success, despite endowments and capabilities that astounded all those who heard him, Richter's career moved slowly. He did not win a single major award until his thirtieth

106

year when he received first prize in a piano competition in Moscow. He then confined his concert work exclusively to the Soviet Union for five years. He was thirty-five before he played outside the Soviet Union for the first time. This took place in 1950 when he was invited to appear at the Prague Festival. For the first time rumors of his greatness began to percolate outside the Iron Curtain, since the Prague Festival had attracted a number of visitors from the Western world, including one or two from the United States. He showed how fantastic his repertory, versatility, memory, and stamina were one season in Berlin when within a few weeks he gave twenty concerts with twenty different programs. Then in 1960, when he was forty-five, he went through the Iron Curtain for the first time by making his initial appearances in the United States.

Richter occupies a four-room sixth-floor apartment just off Moscow's Gorky Street, with his wife, Nina Dorliak, a prominent singer of Lieder and professor at the Moscow Conservatory. One of these rooms is his studio, which houses his two grand pianos (a Steinway and a Bechstein), a recording apparatus with piles upon piles of long-playing records, some paintings on the walls (including one of his own landscapes), an easel, and various *objets d'art* (the most valuable being a fourteenth-century Russian ikon). The Richters also own a modest country home in the warm south on the banks of the Oka River—Richter being particularly partial to the sun and mild weather. His favorite form of transportation is in a modest Citroen car which he himself drives.

He is a temperamental and moody artist who will not play when he is not in the mood. That is why at some concerts he may be overgenerous with encores while at others he refuses to play even one. That is also why, on occasions, he will willingly tolerate a breathless and overtaxing concert schedule and on other occasions will refuse to give a single concert within the space of a few months. But he insists that all this is not just caprice or whim but "a question of how I feel. Good performance requires the creation of a certain tension between pianist and audience. It sometimes happens that I feel too casual, too self-assured. For example, once when I was playing in a foreign capital I went right from the railroad station to the concert hall. The result was an absence of that state of tension which I require of myself if I am to play effectively."

Like so many musicians, Richter is a passionate lover of nature. His favored form of escape from the stresses and strains of concert work is to hike for miles at a time in the country. He also finds release from tensions in painting, his favorite form being landscapes in water colors.

He practices the piano from three to ten hours a day, depending upon his moods and inner urges. He has been known to come home from a concert and then practice for the rest of that night. He opposes specialization of any kind as a performer, preferring to devote himself to all types of music rather than to any single composer, period, or school. "A pianist," he has said, "should be able to play Max Reger one night and George Gershwin the next. My favorite composer is the one I am working on or performing at the time." There are some significant works which he himself may value highly and like hearing but which he will not perform because for one reason or another he does not feel he can do them justice; and there are other works he may not particularly like but which he will include in his programs because they offer him a challenge and permit him "to discover yet another aspect of

108

[my] talent and convey it to the audience."

On some points he is both dogmatic and intransigent: He will never play transcriptions of Bach's organ works or Schubert's songs, however good or valuable these may be. He insists upon playing new music all the time and is particularly partial to the presentation of world *premières*.

DAVID OISTRAKH

[1908-   ]

LONG BEFORE David Oistrakh came to the United States for the first time he was known both through his recordings and by word-of-mouth reputation. The consensus of critical opinion held that Oistrakh was the leading violinist in the Soviet Union, and one of the greatest in the world.

The fact that he was the first significant violinist to come from the Soviet Union to tour America made Oistrakh a subject for a good deal of advance publicity. Long before he first set foot on American soil he had become a familiar name, face, and personality to Americans by virtue of extended feature stories in magazines and newspapers.

Oistrakh was no awe-inspiring violin prodigy the way Jascha Heifetz had been—Heifetz having made his debut at the age of six with a phenomenal performance of Mendelssohn's *Violin Concerto*. Oistrakh matured and ripened slowly as an artist. He was born in Odessa on September 30, 1908. His father was a clerk, his mother, a professional singer. When he was five, David began studying the violin with Pytor Stoliarsky. When Stoliarsky was appointed director of the Odessa Conservatory, Oistrakh entered his violin class there.

Stoliarsky, who remained Oistrakh's only teacher, subjected the boy to a rigorous training both in solo performance and in chamber music. By the time Oistrakh was graduated from the Odessa Conservatory in 1926 he had made a number of public appearances in student concerts, but none of these suggested that he was above the usual run-of-the-mill prodigy.

Following his graduation from the Conservatory, Oistrakh still gave few signs that he was eventually to become a world-famous virtuoso. For a while he played the violin in the Odessa Symphony. After that he toured Russia in joint concerts with Ekaterina Geltser, a famous ballerina. A significant turning point came for him in 1927 when he played Glazunov's *Violin Concerto* with the Tia Symphony in Kiev, with the composer himself conducting. Glazunov hailed him then as a violinist of first significance, and stood ready to use his immense influence to further Oistrakh's career. That career now began to gain momentum. In 1928 Oistrakh settled in Moscow, and early the following year he began to establish his reputation with outstanding performances in that city and in Leningrad.

Honors now started coming thick and fast: first prize in a Ukrainian competition held in Kharkov in 1930; first prize in the All-Union Competition in Leningrad in 1934; in 1935, first prize in the Wieniawski competition in Warsaw; and most important of all, first prize in the Queen Elizabeth Competition in Brussels in 1937. His place in the Soviet Union as its foremost violinist was confirmed when in 1942 he was given the Stalin Prize, the highest award the government could bestow in the arts. In later years he gathered many more honors in and out of the Soviet Union. He was given the title of People's Artist of the U.S.S.R. And he was elected an honorary member to several renowned institutions including the Royal

Academy of Music in London, the Academy of Sciences in Berlin, the Santa Cecilia Academy in Rome, and the American Academy of Arts and Sciences in Boston.

His fame now began spreading out in ever-widening circles: in Turkey in 1935, the Scandinavian and the Baltic countries in 1936, France in 1938. In 1951 he scored a sensation at the May Music Festival in Florence, Italy. Three years after that he was invited to play for the conference of foreign ministers in the Soviet embassy in East Berlin. In February 1955 he became the first Soviet musician to concertize in Japan since the end of World War II, and in April of the same year he made a triumphant tour of Germany.

He had been invited to come to the United States as far back as 1939, to perform at the New York World's Fair. But the outbreak of World War II shattered these plans. The American public now had to wait almost two decades to hear him. When they did, David Oistrakh was no longer the violinist of immense promise he had been in the 1930's, but one of even greater fulfillment.

That American debut took place at Carnegie Hall in New York City on November 20, 1955; a second concert was scheduled in the same hall three days later. No sooner had the announcement been made of the two dates when lines began to form outside the Hall. One hour after the tickets had been put on sale they disappeared. Sold-out houses also became the rule wherever Oistrakh played during his six-week tour, whether as a guest of leading orchestras or in recital. In New York it seemed that anybody who had ever held a fiddle and bow in hand was present to listen, from Fritz Kreisler and Nathan Milstein down.

Oistrakh was heard in a large, varied repertory that spanned

113

three centuries—familiar and unfamiliar works; old works and new ones. In New York, on December 21, he played three concertos with the New York Philharmonic (Mozart's *A major*, the Brahms, and the Tchaikovsky). On December 29, once again in New York, he gave the American *première* of a new violin concerto by the leading Soviet composer, Dimitri Shostakovich. (Oistrakh had introduced the work to the world, in Russia, the preceding October.)

Short, chubby, with a round cherubic face that never seemed to lose its placidity, Oistrakh always gave the impression of relaxed and effortless performance. He negotiated bravura passages with dash and brilliance—and with the most deceptive ease—in the best traditions of Russian violin playing. His technique was formidable; his tone was big; his style was majestic; his left hand was capable of lightning precision; his right bow arm was light as a feather.

"The fiddle," said Harold C. Schonberg in *The New York Times*, "is an extension of his hands and he plays it with the ease of one slipping on a pair of old gloves." But it was perhaps in the more thoughtful music that his real supremacy among living violinists became most evident. It was here that he betrayed the breadth and dimension of his profound musicianship; the resiliency with which he could adapt technique and style to the demands of different eras, whether classic, romantic, or modern; the sensitivity of his response to the most subtle nuances, suggestions, and colorations; most of all the way in which his musicianship, imagination, and good taste at all times threw a piercing illumination on the music he was playing. He left no doubt, as Howard Taubman emphasized in *The New York Times*, that "he was one of the outstanding fiddlers of our day. . . . He is a master fiddler by any

114

standards, technical or interpretative."

"As Kreisler used to," reported a critic for *Musical America*, "Oistrakh can hold thousands of listeners in almost agonized concentration with one exquisitely molded and sustained tone, which seems to sum up a lifetime of experience."

Exacting concert schedules that carry him around the world and involve him in more than one hundred performances a year do not keep him from other musical endeavors which Oistrakh regards as no less significant. He feels, for example, that the performance of chamber music is an essential facet of his musical life, without which it could never be a rounded whole. He has, therefore, always performed a good deal of chamber music. In 1935 he toured the Soviet Union in sonata recitals with the pianist Lev Oborin. Later on, with Oborin, he organized a trio that included the cellist Sviatoslav Koussevitzky. Since then Oistrakh has also organized a chamber-music group, of which his trio is the nucleus, which has given subscription concerts in Moscow and Leningrad.

Even more significantly does Oistrakh regard his duties as a professor of the violin at the Moscow Conservatory. He joined the violin faculty of that institution in 1934, and in 1939 he was elevated to professorial rank. His burgeoning virtuoso career notwithstanding—and in spite of the demands that that career makes on both his time and energies—Oistrakh still insists upon assuming a full load as violin teacher. He describes his teaching chores as "a creative laboratory" and insists that his work at the Conservatory reacts favorably to the benefit of his own development as a virtuoso. But even if he himself did not derive such dividends from teaching he would still be devoting a good deal of his time to his students. He feels ever so strongly that it is a moral obligation on his part to "pass on my experience and knowledge to the youth of the younger generation." He takes on some twenty students at a time. Naturally only the cream of the young violinist crop is skimmed for Oistrakh. Oistrakh himself carefully screens each candidate. "I listen to him and if it seems that he has prospects for growth, that he is gifted and won't be lazy, and I am physically able, I take him in. Unfortunately, not all can be taken." His pupils may refer to him informally and affectionately as "David Fydorovoch" but in the classroom they get no quarter and ask for none. Oistrakh is, as might be expected, a martinet; a perfectionist himself, he demands the ultimate in effort and achievement on the part of his students. "Bad! Bad!" he might shout after a pupil has gone through a composition. Then, putting his own violin to chin, he will demonstrate what had gone wrong and show how these faults can best be remedied. "He's a remarkable teacher," one of his pupils, Yuri Mazurkevich, told an interviewer. "He gives you an understanding of the music just like an artist. He's most demanding. And when he doesn't like something or if you repeat stupid mistakes or are not prepared he can be very unpleasant."

Out of Oistrakh's classes have stepped many a violinist who has won significant awards and progressed to distinguished careers. Possibly the most important of these is Oistrakh's own son, Igor. Since Igor's mother is also a fine musician (a graduate student in piano of the Moscow Conservatory) it was only to be expected that music should play a major role in his early life. For a while Igor studied with his father's teacher, Stoliarsky. For a number of years Igor showed little disposition to practice, and consequently made little progress. But during World War II his interest in the violin was suddenly fanned into flame. After some additional study with Stoliarsky, he entered his father's class at the Moscow Conservatory. He then went on to win several distinguished awards, including one in Budapest, and the Wieniawski Contest in Warsaw. After that he forged a truly distinguished career for himself on the concert stage. Father and son have often been heard in duo-violin recitals.

The Oistrakhs occupy an apartment in Moscow and a villa outside the city. When David Oistrakh is free from his concert and teaching commitments—this happens during the summer— he leaves for the seashore (often to Estonia). There he diverts himself by swimming, motoring, playing chess and an occasional game of tennis, and pampering his brood of Siamese cats. But even during this recreation period there is a good deal of work to be done. For this is the time Oistrakh reserves for the study of new scores. Oistrakh has always been a passionate propagandist for modern Soviet composers; he never relaxes his efforts to introduce their latest violin compositions. Miaskovsky, Khatchaturian, Shostakovich, Prokofiev have all written major works for him. Oistrakh also keeps in touch with contemporary music outside the Soviet Union through the printed page, but mostly through recordings. Wherever he settles for a comfortable stay he insists upon having near him a hi-fi set and piles of long-playing records— both for study and for recreation. For as far as Oistrakh is concerned if he cannot make music, or teach others to make it, then what he likes best of all is to listen to it.

MSTISLAV ROSTROPOVICH

[1927–   ]

$\mathcal{T}$HE SOUNDS, the tonal visions a composer tries to put down
on paper are at the mercy of the performer who brings them
to life. It is on the virtuoso's dedication and faithful adherence
to the intentions of the printed page—as well as to his technical facility and musicianship—that a musical creator must de-
pend implicitly if audiences are to hear what he had in heart
and mind. Too often a virtuoso is not the unobstructed channel
through which a creator's ideas flow. Too often a virtuoso tries
to superimpose his own ideas upon those of the composer by
changing the rhythm, introducing uncalled-for rubatos, alter-
ing tempo. The virtuoso may call these personal revisions
"interpretation," but they are really nothing of the kind at all.
Interpretation in its truest and finest sense occurs when a
virtuoso can realize the completest, fullest, and subtlest intents
of a composer; when he can sublimate his own ideas and idiosyncrasies to the demands of the music he is performing.

It is sometimes possible to measure the greatness of a performing artist by the eagerness with which leading composers
write major works for him. A good many significant composers
of our time look upon Mstislav Rostropovich as the ideal inter-

preter of their cello literature. When Rostropovich plays, you sense he has penetrated to the inmost depths of a given work and lifted from it every possible meaning the music has. You are never made forcefully conscious of the artistry of the virtuoso; it is the artistry of the composer that seems to compel all your attention. This is why so many composers have written major works for Rostropovich. These composers are assured that their compositions will be played the way they were written, and not the way a virtuoso thinks they should have been written.

Already early in his career Rostropovich found composers ready and willing to produce for him large-scale compositions. When, in 1945, Rostropovich entered a contest in Moscow, he was required by the rules of the competition to perform a concerto by the contemporary Soviet composer, Miaskovsky. Miaskovsky was so impressed by Rostropovich's performance (which, incidentally, won the first prize for the cellist) that he proceeded without delay to write for him a new cello sonata, which Rostropovich introduced in 1949. Prokofiev was the next important Soviet composer to write a sonata for Rostropovich, its *première* given in Moscow with Sviatoslav Richter at the piano. Subsequently, Prokofiev was stimulated by Rostropovich's re-creative art to produce for him a cello concerto and a Sinfonia Concertante. (Prokofiev did not live to complete his concerto, and Rostropovich finished it for him.) The dedication page reads: "Dedicated to the outstanding talent, Mstislav Rostropovich, with grateful remembrance of our joint work on this concerto."

Shostakovich, another major Soviet composer, also wrote a concerto for Rostropovich, with the cellist performed in Moscow and Leningrad. For Rostropovich, Khatchaturian created the *Concerto Rhapsody*, a work many critics regard as one of the composer's finest. Glière, still another Soviet composer, also wrote for Rostropovich—and so did England's leading composer, Benjamin Britten. Britten's *Cello Sonata*, written with Rostropovich in mind, was given its *première* at the Aldeburgh Festival in England in 1961, with Rostropovich playing the cello and the composer at the piano; after that Rostropovich and Sviatoslav Richter gave successful performances of this sonata all over the Soviet Union. More recently Britten produced for the cellist an even more exciting composition in the *Symphony for Cello and Orchestra* which was introduced by Rostropovich in Moscow on March 12, 1964.

The reason that Rostropovich is such a favorite of modern composers when they write for the cello is because he is "no dazzler, no hypnotist, no demon of the bow," as Jay S. Harrison once wrote of him in the *New York Herald Tribune*. "Nor does he try to be." His technique, of course, is commanding and supreme. But he "conceals his technical abilities. . . . Had he the desire to buzz about the strings frantically, make brilliant splashes of sound and release all manner of lush effects, he is, no doubt, fully capable of doing so. But the meretricious is clearly not his way. He is sober, serious, intense, and devoted."

His tone is comparatively small; he scrupulously avoids smothering a phrase with luscious vibrations or a swell of sensual sound. "His preference," Howard Taubman explained in *The New York Times*, "is evidently for a wide range of nuance within a relatively limited compass of soft to loud. . . . The impression is one of delicacy and refinement. . . . He plays . . . with inwardness and subtlety. . . . Refinement is his natural style." Amplifying on these remarks Paul Henry Lang added in the *New York Herald Tribune*: "He is the 'musician first' type of virtuoso."

Rostropovich grew up in a home where there was music all the time. His father was a professional cellist and teacher—a pupil of the renowned Karl Davidoff, often described as the founder of the Russian school of cello performance. His mother was an excellent pianist. Informal concerts were a favored form of entertainment in the Rostropovich household. As far back as his memory could reach into his childhood, Rostropovich remembers the sounds of great music surrounding him, and the joy which music making brought its makers.

Mstislav was born in Baku, Azerbaijan, on the Caspian Sea, on March 27, 1927. When he was four, his father was appointed teacher of the cello at the Gnessin School of Music in Moscow. The family, therefore, made the move to the Soviet capital. At the age of five Mstislav started to learn to play the piano by himself, and was soon able to perform so proficiently that he could participate in the family concerts. His father started giving him lessons on the cello when Mstislav was eight, combining these with instruction in composition three years later.

From his seventh to his fourteenth years Mstislav attended the Preparatory Seven Years' School in Moscow. This was a private institution for children of unusual talent in music where they could receive a comprehensive academic education as well as one in music. By the time he was fourteen Mstislav was ready to concentrate on music exclusively. He now enrolled in the Moscow Conservatory where he studied the cello with Semeon Kozolupoff (also a Davidoff pupil). While attending the Conservatory Rostropovich completed a number of large compositions for orchestra and for the cello, as well as several piano concertos. He also appeared frequently in sonata recitals with Sviatoslav Richter, and in trio performances with Emil

Gilels and Leonid Kogan.

World War II and the Nazi invasion of the Soviet Union temporarily halted Rostropovich's music study. With the Nazi guns booming at the gates of Moscow, the Rostropovich family was evacuated to the Ural Mountains. There, in comparative safety from the ravages of war, Rostropovich continued to work by himself in the perfection of his technique and in mastering a repertory. Finally, the war ended, he could continue his studies at the Moscow Conservatory where he completed a three-year postgraduate course in 1948. Meanwhile, he had won two important competitions for cellists, the first being the All-Union Contest in the Soviet Union, and the other at the International Youth Festival in Prague.

His studies now ended, Rostropovich embarked on a dual career in music. As a cello virtuoso he appeared in concerts throughout the Soviet Union. When free from his concert commitments he devoted himself to teaching the cello at the Moscow Conservatory.

He gave evidence of his truly exceptional gifts as a cellist for the first time in Moscow in 1951 with two remarkable concerts devoted to all of Bach's solo cello suites and sonatas. Two years later he was heard in Beethoven's five cello sonatas on a single program. He was also being heard and admired outside the Soviet Union. In 1951 he appeared at the Florence May Music Festival. Howard Taubman, then the music critic of *The New York Times*, heard him there at that time and reported back to his paper: "Rostropovich . . . was . . . first class. His tone was . . . clean and accurate, and his musicianship was searching, particularly in Bach's unaccompanied *C minor Suite*. His musical style seemed to be ardent and intense, and it was only in the short encore pieces that he showed he could be light in touch." Appearances in other European music centers followed—notably in London and Paris—and the accolades kept accumulating.

On April 4, 1956, Rostropovich made his bow in the United States with a recital in Carnegie Hall, New York City. Three weeks later he gave the American *première* of the *Second Cello Concerto* which Prokofiev had written for him. The American critics outdid one another in singing his praises. "Rostropovich," summed up Jay S. Harrison in the *Herald Tribune*, "is a cellist of true stature. Better still—he is a musician of grandeur." Some went so far as to single him out as the most logical successor to the crown worn so long by Pablo Casals, the greatest cellist of the twentieth century. Not yet thirty, Rostropovich had joined the elect of the concert world.

Tall, lean, bespectacled, Rostropovich is hardly likely to attract second notice when he is away from his cello. In spite of his successes, he is a shy young man who is self-conscious, withdrawn, diffident. He is married to a famous singer, Galina Vishnevskaya; their Philips recordings of Moussorgsky's *Songs and Dances of Death* and Prokofiev's song cycle, *Anna Akhmatova*, each received the Grand Prix du Disque in Paris. To stay as much as possible with her husband, Galina has reduced her own concert appearances to a minimum.

Separated from his music, Rostropovich is most interested in mechanics and engineering. He devours technical journals through which he tries to keep in touch with latest developments. Aware of his interest, French music lovers presented him with a model of a French express train when he came to Paris for the first time in 1951; and this has since become one of his most prized possessions.

DANIEL BARENBOIM

[1942–   ]

*D*URING A VISIT to Israel in 1962 this writer was invited to attend an audition for scholarships for young performing artists in Tel Aviv. For several days a distinguished jury headed by Israel's leading composer, Paul Ben-Haim, listened patiently to some four hundred young artists. Some, including girls, were in military uniform. Many were mere children. One or two were tots. Some had acquired their past musical training under the most difficult circumstances imaginable, since they had come out of collective farms (*kibbutzim*) where often a single piano, and very little printed music, had to serve the needs of many. To some of the contestants these scholarships offered the only possible means of further instruction.

One after another these young musicians appeared on the stage. They announced their own names, then the titles of the compositions they were about to play. Then with quiet and professional despatch they went through their performance. The repertory at these auditions was wide and varied, ranging from Johann Sebastian Bach and Domenico Scarlatti to Scriabin and Prokofiev. The level of achievement was high, even if the conditions under which these young people had developed had been far from ideal. Knowing as I did how some of these youngsters had acquired their training, I felt that the results at times were incredible.

It was the intention of the jury to provide one hundred scholarships—which represented all the money available at that time. But since more than one hundred and sixty of these youngsters had received a grade of 90 per cent or more, the judges decided they simply would have to find ways and means of increasing the number of scholarships to one hundred and fifty. All these scholarships would provide for piano study in Israel, mostly in conservatories, but occasionally with highly qualified private teachers.

In a few years' time, after these scholarship winners had received extensive training, they would be able to audition a second time—for the privilege of being able to continue and conclude their studies outside Israel in some of the world's great music institutions. These advanced scholarships were first instituted in 1954-1955 by the America Israel Cultural Foundation. For the next half-dozen years or so fifty were selected to complete their musical education either in Europe or America—not only in piano, violin, and cello, but also in voice, conducting, and musicology.

By this process, within the brief period of its stormy existence, Israel has been able to develop a number of artists now capable of enriching the concert-going experiences of music lovers the world over.

One of these is the pianist Daniel Barenboim. He was one of the first to get the advanced scholarship for musical study outside Israel from the America Israel Cultural Foundation. Barenboim was born in Buenos Aires, Argentina, on November 6, 1942. Both parents were musicians. In early childhood

Daniel received piano instruction first from his mother and later from his father. He gave his first concert when he was seven, in Buenos Aires. The audience proved so enthusiastic that the child was compelled to give seven encores. The only reason he stopped after his seventh encore was that by then his entire repertory had been exhausted. A number of appearances in Buenos Aires followed. Igor Markevitch, a distinguished conductor in France, became so impressed with his playing that he urged the child to come to Salzburg and continue his music study at the Mozarteum—Markevitch then being a member of that faculty in the department of conducting. In 1952 Barenboim played the *D minor Concerto* of Mozart in Salzburg. He was then allowed by the city officials to give a concert on Mozart's own spinet, the first time in twenty-five years that anyone had been permitted to touch that keyboard. Barenboim later appeared in recitals and as guest artist with orchestras. "Daniel Barenboim," said Wilhelm Furtwängler, one of the world's greatest conductors, "is a phenomenon; his musical and technical capacities are equally amazing."

After an extensive period of music study in Salzburg (piano with Edwin Fischer, one of the most revered pianists in Germany and Austria; chamber music with Enrico Mainardi; conducting with Markevitch), the young Barenboim came to Vienna where, among several appearances, he gave an all-American music concert. An Italian tour followed where besides his concert engagements he made his first recordings. A sweep across Europe and the Near East led through Milan, Tel Aviv, Jerusalem, Haifa, Athens, Zurich, Bern, Basel, Amsterdam, and Paris. In January 1956 Barenboim made his debut in England by appearing as soloist with the Royal Philharmonic in Mozart's *A major Concerto*. The critic of the London *Times* said: "There is no doubt about his pianistic ability, which is prodigious for his age, nor about his musicality, for his use of a wide range of tone was always à propos."

Meanwhile, the Barenboim family had settled permanently in Israel and had become Israeli citizens. As an Israeli, Daniel Barenboim was selected by the America Israel Cultural Foundation for one of its first scholarships for music study abroad. In 1956, therefore, Barenboim studied first with Nadia Boulanger in Paris (composition), then at the Academia Chigiani in Siena, and finally with Carlo Zecchi at the renowned Santa Cecilia Academy in Rome where he became one of the youngest musicians in the history of that institution to receive its diploma. He also won an important Italian piano competition, the Alfred Casella contest in Naples.

Now the fully-ripened artist, Barenboim was signed by the management of S. Hurok for extended concert appearances. In January 1957 Barenboim made his American debut in Carnegie Hall as soloist with the Symphony of the Air conducted by Leopold Stokowski. The *New York Herald Tribune* called him "every inch a miniature master" and the New York *Post* described him as "a remarkable young artist." When, a year later, Barenboim gave his first New York recital, Howard Taubman said in *The New York Times*: "His future can be as big as he chooses to make it. Already exceptional as a teen-ager, he could become one of the major virtuosos of tomorrow."

Within a short period of time Taubman's "tomorrow" had become "today." During the next few years Barenboim made several more coast-to-coast tours of the United States (his seventh taking place in 1964–1965). He also toured South America, Europe, the Near East, Australia, and New Zealand.

His cycles devoted to all the piano sonatas of Beethoven and Mozart have become artistic events of the first significance wherever he chose to give them. "Few young artists," said *Time* magazine in 1962, "can muster the depths of thought and feeling that seem to come to him naturally." After Barenboim had appeared as soloist with Sir John Barbirolli, the eminent conductor called him "the greatest talent I have come across for many years. . . . His kind of musicality is very rare." Pointing no less a firm finger at Barenboim's remarkable gifts is the winning of the Harriet Cohen-Paderewski Centenary Prize in London, probably the most highly esteemed award England can bestow on a pianist.

SHMUEL ASHKENASI

[1941–   ]

DAVID BAR-ILIAN

[1930–   ]

$\mathcal{T}$HE YOUNG Israeli violinist, Shmuel Ashkenasi, is an artist for whom winning a scholarship from the America Israel Cultural Foundation has proved the steppingstone toward an impressive virtuoso career.

Born in Tel Aviv, Israel, on January 11, 1941, Ashkenasi began studying the violin at the Israel Music Academy with Ilona Feher when he was eight. Three years later Ashkenasi made an impressive concert debut by appearing as soloist with the Kol Israel Orchestra affiliated with the Israeli radio. In 1955 he won the scholarship that made it possible for him to come to the United States for the first time. When he auditioned for Efrem Zimbalist, director of the Curtis Institute in Philadelphia (and himself once a renowned concert violinist), the veteran musician not only accepted Ashkenasi into the Curtis Institute, but even took him along to his summer home in Rockport, Maine, for private study. During the next few years Ashkenasi spent his winters in Philadelphia at the Curtis Institute and his summers with Zimbalist at Rockport. During this period he won first prize in a contest for violinists in Washington, D.C., which brought him appearances with the National Symphony in Washington, Howard Mitchell conducting. In 1959 the Curtis Institute sponsored Ashkenasi's trip to Brussels, so that he might compete in the world-famous Queen Elizabeth Competition. He did not win first prize, although he did manage to be one of the finalists.

Still a student at Curtis, and sponsored by it, Ashkenasi was sent to Moscow in 1962 to participate in the second International Tchaikovsky Competition. (The first of these competitions, that for pianists, was the one in which Van Cliburn had taken first prize.) Despite the fact that because of a breakdown in transportation, Ashkenasi had been compelled to walk several miles to appear at the semifinals, he made a brilliant showing. He was given one of the longest standing ovations Muscovites remembered. In the end, he captured second prize. Even though that first prize went to somebody else, Ashkenasi's performance had been so brilliant that S. Hurok immediately took him under his managerial wing for a world tour. Extended appearances in the Soviet Union and Israel came after that. Then, when Ashkenasi had graduated from the Curtis Institute in 1963, he made his first extended tour of the United States, followed by his first tour of Europe. "His tone is silky, elastic, and of great beauty," said the critic of the Berlin *Die Welt*, "and he is capable of remarkable pianissimi at the top of the scale. Technically he is beyond reproach. Surely he is on his way to becoming a master."

David Bar-Ilian, pianist, is one of the most significant of Israel's virtuosos. He can trace back both his Israeli background and his musical heritage three generations. His grandfather and father were both Palestinians, and both had been highly accomplished musicians, the former was a creator of liturgical music, and the latter a gifted pianist.

Born in Haifa in 1930, David demonstrated his gift for music from infancy on. When he was six he was taken to his first concert, given by the then newly founded Palestine Symphony (later to be renamed the Israel Philharmonic). The conductor was Arturo Toscanini. "I was hypnotized by that concert," Bar-Ilian later recalled, "and immediately begged my parents to let me begin lessons."

His music study started in Haifa, and soon was supplemented by visits to Europe where he could absorb its musical and cultural traditions. A scholarship finally brought him to the United States for study at the Julliard School of Music in New York. These studies were interrupted when Israel became involved in its war for liberation. Bar-Ilian returned to his native land and, joining the underground military (Hagannah), fought side by side with his compatriots at great personal risk. With Israel liberated and become a state, and with peace restored, David Bar-Ilian could return to music. He came back to the United States where his piano study was completed at the Mannes School of Music.

His professional career began with two successful concerts in London and with the winning of the Coronation Year Medal in England for distinguished artistic achievement. This, in turn, led to his first tour of the United States in 1959–1960, climaxed by a successful first appearance with the New York

Philharmonic in January 1960, Dimitri Mitropoulos conducting.

The rapidity with which his career now unfolded in the music centers of the world was emphasized during a two-month period in the fall of 1961 in three different cities. First, on September 14 and 15, he was a guest artist with the Berlin Philharmonic when he played Beethoven's *Third Piano Concerto*, Karl Boehm conducting. It took a good deal of soul-searching for Bar-Ilian to accept this engagement. He knew he would be severely attacked in his own country for appearing in Berlin, since so many Israelis—remembering their former suffering in Nazi Germany—favored a boycott of Germany in all fields of endeavor. But Bar-Ilian was personally convinced that the time had come to try to pave the way for good will and understanding between Israel and the new Germany; that it was time to forget the scars and wounds caused by the Nazi regime and World War II. He found to his delight that a good many people in Germany agreed with him. Berlin gave him a rousing welcome, and after his performance, an unforgettable ovation. "He lived each phrase, and illuminated the expressive value of the work, with exactness and deep understanding," wrote the critic of the Berlin *Kurier*.

Six weeks later Bar-Ilian was called to Amsterdam to substitute for the distinguished Soviet pianist, Emil Gilels, who had been scheduled to appear with the Concertgebouw Orchestra but was indisposed. Bar-Ilian came, played the *E-flat major Concerto* of Liszt, and conquered. If there was any disappointment in the substitution of Bar-Ilian for Gilels it was felt neither in the auditorium nor the next day in the press. The *Algemeen Handelsblad* called his performance "a shattering event" and added that "no one could have imagined a worthier substitute for Gilels than Bar-Ilian."

Then before the year of 1961 was over Bar-Ilian was heard as soloist with the Berlin Philharmonic under Karl Boehm during its visit to New York on its third American tour. Once again Bar-Ilian played Beethoven's *Third Piano Concerto.* "Another ovation went to the Israeli pianist, David Bar-Ilian," wrote the critic of the New York *World Telegram and Sun.* "Here is an attractive keyboard personality of poetic leanings and gentle fingers. . . . Mr. Bar-Ilian always played like a well-bred artist who took his time and never sought to impress by the simple device of raising his voice."

His career has been flowering ever since then. During the seasons of 1962–1963 and 1963–1964 he made his first appearance with several of America's greatest orchestras including the Philadelphia, the Cleveland, the Cincinnati, and the Indianapolis. He was invited to appear with the Baltimore Symphony during its tour of the Southwest when he was heard in twenty-four cities. He filled engagements in Holland, Germany, France, Denmark, England, and South America. During the summer of 1963 he participated in an all-Mozart program at the famous Berkshire Music Festival in Tanglewood, Lenox, Massachusetts. In March 1964, when the Cincinnati Orchestra paid a visit to Carnegie Hall in New York, it had Bar-Ilian as its soloist in the *G minor Concerto* of Mendelssohn.

Since Bar-Ilian is now called upon to fill many engagements in the United States throughout the year, he has acquired a permanent apartment in New York City, near Central Park. David's wife, Wilmetta, is an American pianist from Twin Falls, Idaho; he first met her at the Aspen (Colorado) Music Festival. She gave up the concert stage when she married Bar-

Ilian to enter upon a completely new career, as food specialist—designing menus and recipes for restaurants and magazines. The rest of her time is devoted to the raising of two children, a daughter, and a son.

But Bar-Ilian has by no means cut his ties to his native land. He returns regularly not only to visit his family but also to give concerts, make radio appearances, and perform with the Israel Philharmonic and the Kol Yisroel Orchestra. His wife, also, has made a contribution to the young Near East democracy. Under the sponsorship of the International Cooperation Administration of the United States State Department she has conducted a survey of the food situation in restaurants and hotels in Israel in an effort to develop a "characteristic Israeli cuisine."

WHITTEMORE AND LOWE

[1916–   ]   [1917–   ]

GOLD AND FIZDALE

[1919–   ]   [1920–   ]

FROM THE TIME composers began writing music for the keyboard they produced literature for two pianos: Giles Farnaby in England in the sixteenth century; Bernardo Pasquini in Italy, François Couperin-le-Grand in France, and the great Johann Sebastian Bach in Germany, in the seventeenth; and Wolfgang Amadeus Mozart in the eighteenth. But the two-piano team is a comparatively recent concert-hall attraction. In the more distant past two piano virtuosos would sometimes join up to perform works such as the Bach or Mozart two-piano concertos in gala concerts. Such performances were given in the nineteenth century by Franz Liszt and Frédéric Chopin, and by Felix Mendelssohn and his sister, Fanny. But two pianists who devote themselves completely and exclusively to each other in the presentation of two-piano music are actually a twentieth-century development.

One of the earliest such teams to become a part of the American concert scene was Guy Maier and Lee Pattison, who made their debut in New York in 1916 and then continued to concertize together for the next fourteen years. After that, other two-piano combinations emerged and toured the music world. The foremost of these were Bartlett and Robertson, who gave their first concerts in London in 1927 and in New York in 1928; and Luboschutz and Nemenoff and Vronsky and Babin, each of whom made a first transcontinental American tour in 1937–1938.

A successful two-piano team must comprise two individuals whose two hearts beat as one, whose two minds function as one, and whose individual artistic sensibilities must blend into a single, inextricable personality. In short, a two-piano team must be—as has often been said—four hands with one mind.

Since the end of World War II two significant American two-piano teams have become prominent: Whittemore and Lowe and Gold and Fizdale. In each instance the individuals are remarkable pianists and outstanding musicians. But one of the reasons that each of these teams has proved to possess a single artistic personality is because with each pair the two men have similar diversions, interests, outlooks, and enthusiasms. Thus as a team each is able to function as a single entity; and this is one of the reasons for their success.

Arthur Whittemore and Jack Lowe were born a year apart: Whittemore, son of a famous football coach, in Vermillion, South Dakota, on October 23, 1916; Jack Lowe in Aurora, near Denver, Colorado, on December 25, 1917. Before their respective paths met and joined each had given proof of his musical capabilities and had received a sound musical

138

training. Whittemore began to study the piano at five, wrote his first compositions at six, and at twelve was already working as organist at a local Congregational Church. For a long time academic and music study was pursued with equal industry, the latter with private teachers. Upon being graduated from the University of South Dakota in 1934, Whittemore came to the Eastman School of Music in Rochester, New York, on a teaching fellowship. In 1935 he was made director of music at the University of Rochester College for Men.

It was at the Eastman School of Music that he first met and befriended Jack Lowe. Curiously enough, Lowe had received his early musical training on the violin rather than the piano, and had proved so adept on that instrument that he was able to make his debut while he was still a child, and at sixteen to join the violin section of the Denver Symphony. Later on, as a student at the Colorado State Teachers College, he earned his living playing both the violin and the piano at summer resorts. Suddenly he found the piano more attractive than the violin. He now concentrated on studying that instrument, making sufficient progress to win a scholarship for piano study at the Eastman School of Music. In 1935 he was made Whittemore's assistant at the College for Men. There he helped Whittemore train the university glee club which, still in 1935, won a national award in a contest among one hundred and fifty participating groups.

They became close friends, drawn together not only by their professional ties and interests but also by the fact that they seemed to like the same things away from music, such as swimming and sailing. They also seemed to have the same outlook on most things. When, therefore, Whittemore was invited by his aunt to stay at her home in Puerto Rico in 1935 he wanted his friend Jack Lowe to accompany him there. To inveigle his aunt into giving Lowe an invitation, he concocted a story that they were a two-piano team and therefore had to travel together to keep up their practicing. The ruse worked—even better than Whittemore had expected. When Whittemore and Lowe came to Puerto Rico they discovered that the aunt had arranged for them to give a two-piano concert in San Juan. Rather than confess he had lied, Whittemore persuaded Lowe to begin an intensive period of two-piano practice for the purpose of filling the engagement. Since they had no two-piano music with them, they went to work at the same time making transcriptions of familiar musical classics. The concert they finally gave was such a huge success—and they derived such delight in collaborating in the making of music—that then and there they decided to become a two-piano team.

For a while, beginning with 1938, they gave daily concerts on two pianos over a radio station in Pittsburgh. In 1940 they made their New York concert debut with a performance at Town Hall. During World War II, with both men serving in the Navy, they performed extensively in hospitals, at army bases, and in combat areas, giving more than seven hundred concerts.

Their professional career as a two-piano team went into high gear as soon as they left the service. In the first year and a half following their separation from the Navy in 1946 they gave more than one hundred concerts. After that they toured the world, made phonograph recordings, and were heard over TV. In all media they established themselves as one of the most highly esteemed two-piano combinations in the world.

There is hardly a major symphony orchestra in the United States that has not invited them as guest artists: there is no important radio or TV program featuring live music that has not recuited them for broadcasts. They became the first classical instrumentalists to have their own TV show, a five-day-a-week telecast over the Mutual network; more recently they have prepared a series of film shorts for television programs all over the country. They have also become the most successful two-piano team to make recordings; they belong to that highly limited and elite circle of serious musicians who have sold more than a million disks.

Wherever they are heard, Whittemore and Lowe never fail to command the admiration and enthusiasm of discriminating music lovers, be it in a metropolis such as New York, or a lesser community in Missouri or Texas. The critic of *The New York Times* said of their performance of Francis Poulenc's *Concerto for Two Pianos:* "One could hardly imagine the concerto being better played. It had refinement, wit, spontaneity, and sweetness. . . . There was a rare singleness of concept in the . . . partnership. The teamwork was perfect, but there was no sense of mechanical precision." In Indianapolis a critic wrote: "Whittemore and Lowe have attained perfect coordination in two decades. Their tonal balance is uncanny. Phrases from the two pianos flow as if they were phrases from a single instrument. This isn't instinct. It is sensitivity plus hours of practice, plus agreement on interpretation." In St. Joseph, Missouri, the critic said: "Virility, versatility, and virtuosity are only three words describing Whittemore and Lowe's duo piano performance. . . . Other applicable 'V' adjectives are verve, vigor, and vivacity." In Green Bay, Wisconsin, the critic reported: "Both are highly skilled, sensitive musicians with impressive technique and a high degree of coordination so esssential to fine two-piano teamwork. It is an exacting art which, after nearly twenty-five years, is nearly second nature to them."

One of the greatest problems facing a two-piano team is that of repertory. Music for two pianos may go far back in music history, but it is at best not plentiful—though it does include some unqualified masterworks. In any event, it is hardly possible to fill up program after program exclusively on music that had originally been written for two pianos. To fill in the gap, many musicians have transcribed music, originally created for other instruments, for two pianists. Transcriptions now form a basic part of almost every two-piano recital. In this activity Whittemore and Lowe have been particularly active, having made more than two hundred and fifty such transcriptions, including classics, semi-classical numbers, and even popular songs.

Gold and Fizdale have also been indefatigable in their efforts to enlarge the repertory of two-piano music. They have commissioned more than twenty important contemporary composers to write new works for them—including Francis Poulenc, Darius Milhaud, and Georges Auric of France, and Virgil Thomson and Ned Rorem in the United States. The tolerance of this duo-piano team to all styles of modern music is proved by the fact that it has even introduced *avant-garde* works by John Cage and compositions in the jazz idiom by Dave Brubeck. In addition to asking leading creative figures to prepare new works for them, Gold and Fizdale have been responsible for reviving works that, for one reason or another, have fallen by the wayside and have been forgotten: Schu-

bert's wonderful *Grand Duo*, for example, or Debussy's *Épi-
graphes antiques* or Béla Bartók's *Sonata for Two Pianos and
Percussion*. Gold and Fizdale have also searched in libraries
the world over for music that might be lying in discard. Thus
they came up with exciting works by Mendelssohn (two un-
published concertos for two pianos) and Schumann (the
Spanische Liebeslieder for two pianos and vocal quartet)
which even some musicologists had not known had existed.

"Like all hams," they once told an interviewer for *Musical
America*, "we want our audiences to like us. People want to
be amused, and our duty is to amuse, and not to bore. So in
programming modern music we want to be far out enough
for our own amusement but not too far out for the various
tastes of our public. . . . Ironically, we find that presenting
older, unfamiliar works holds many of the same problems as
performing modern pieces. Musical styles and epochs have
vogues. New music and newly discovered older music are
judged and treated alike, categorized in clichés by the public
and the critics. These preconceived notions about music plus
those about duo-piano performance traditions are our biggest
obstacles." To which the interviewer added the following
pithy comment: "But anyone who has heard Gold and Fizdale
knows the duo has little to worry about."

Gold and Fizdale share an expansive apartment in New
York City, fitted out with three grand pianos. They have
mutual friends and enjoy an active social life together. Both
are omniverous readers of literature; they always carry along
with them a miniature library whenever they go on tour.
Both are excellent cooks, and are avid collectors of antiques,
glass paintings, and other objects of artistic value and interest.
Both are passionate sight-seeers. Both enjoy going to the

theater and ballet, and both are interested in horticulture. Not only their avocations and interests follow parallel lines, but even their early lives and careers. Both came from Russian parentage; both were child prodigies; each started studying the piano at the age of six. Arthur Gold was born in Toronto, Canada, on February 6, 1919; Robert Fizdale in Chicago, Illinois, on April 12, 1920. When Gold was three years old he was already able to play the piano by ear, well enough to accompany his sister, a singer. Three years later he began studying the piano intensively. Advanced music study took place at the Juilliard School of Music where he met and befriended a fellow student, Robert Fizdale, who also had shown remarkable gifts at the piano from early childhood.

They began playing together at two pianos while still attending Juilliard, and soon came to the realization that two-piano music was the area they wished to cultivate—together. They now say that their first consideration had been the fact that a career as solo piano virtuoso meant continual travels alone, and each was too gregarious to look with favor on a lifetime of such repeated loneliness. But it was their first sessions at two pianos that sealed their musical marriage, for it was then that they came to realize that in artistic temperament, musical outlook, and interpretative ideas they thought and felt alike.

They made their official debut as a two-piano team with a recital in Town Hall, New York City, on February 15, 1946. Virgil Thomson said in the *New York Herald Tribune:* "Duo-pianism reached heights hitherto unknown to the art." Their debut in Europe took place three and a half years after that, with a recital at Salle Gaveau in Paris on June 24, 1949. Upon performing for the first time in England, four years later, they were dubbed by the critic of the London *Times* as "the world's best two-piano team."

Since their first appearances in New York, Paris, and London, Gold and Fizdale have circled the musical globe several times; have appeared as soloists with the world's greatest orchestras; have been heard over radio and television; have made notable recordings. Accolades of all kinds have come their way, but there are two which they treasure particularly. One of these is a letter from Francis Poulenc, distinguished twentieth-century French composer, upon receiving a copy of their recording of his *Concerto for Two Pianos and Orchestra*, which they made with the New York Philharmonic, Leonard Bernstein conducting. Poulenc wrote: "Your performance of the *Concerto*, like that of Horowitz of my *Toccata*, is the one for posterity." The other honor came to them in September 1962 when they were invited by William Schuman, the director of Lincoln Center in New York, to give a recital during the Gala Opening Week of Philharmonic Hall. This was the first piano music heard in that new auditorium.

JULIAN BREAM

[1933–   ]

Concerts by a classical guitar, like those by two-piano
teams, are basically a twentieth-century innovation. This is
so, even though there were a number of distinguished guitar
virtuosos before 1900. Niccolò Paganini, one of the greatest
violin virtuosos of all time, was also a gifted performer on the
guitar, and so was the French Romantic composer, Hector
Berlioz. A Spaniard named Fernando Sor gave such extraordinary guitar concerts in Paris and London in the nineteenth
century that for a while that instrument had a genuine vogue
among serious music lovers. Despite these facts—and despite
the fact that some good music has been written for the guitar
by Paganini, Schubert, and Sor—the instrument, its performer,
and its music disappeared completely from the concert hall
for many years. The guitar was heard mainly in popular music, especially in the popular music of Spain where it became
a native instrument for performances of and accompaniment
to folk songs, and as the musical background for folk dances.

It was in Spain, in the twentieth century, that the guitar
returned triumphantly to the concert stage. This happened

with Andrès Segovia, a remarkable musician whose artistry and technical skill—and whose effective transcriptions for the guitar—brought him to the front rank of performing artists, regardless of instrument. In concerts, first in Spain (the first one taking place in Granada in 1909), then in South America, then throughout Europe, and finally in the United States (where he made a sensational debut in New York in January 1928), Segovia reinstated the guitar to such importance in the concert world that several major modern composers began writing sonatas and concertos for it. For more than a quarter of a century Segovia filled concert halls to capacity as he played masterworks by Johann Sebastian Bach, Haydn, Mendelssohn, and other classical masters together with the serious Spanish works of Tor, Turina, and Ponce, and modern music by Heitor Villa-Lobos, Mario Castelnuovo-Tedesco, and Albert Roussel. Single-handedly, Segovia proved conclusively—as Santiago Kastner noted in Grove's *Dictionary of Music and Musicians* (fifth edition)—"that the guitar has a place as a solo concert instrument" and that Segovia "achieves on it an intensity of expression and depth . . . [creating] an entirely new technique of guitar playing which broke in many respects with the classical Spanish tradition."

Segovia's influence and success were responsible for the founding of a new school of guitar virtuosos, primarily in Spain, but in other countries as well. One of these performers, who by now has become a fixture in the world's concert auditorium, comes from England. He is Julian Bream, who derived his early encouragement and guidance from Segovia.

Julian Bream was born in London on July 15, 1933. Since his father played the guitar, the child Julian was early given lessons on that instrument. By the time he was twelve Julian played the guitar in an ensemble in London. The president of the Society of Guitarists in London took notice of him and took him on as pupil. For three years Bream was given a thorough training on the guitar. Then, when he was fifteen, he received a full-time scholarship at the Royal College of Music in London where he penetrated deeper into the world of serious music through studies of harmony, counterpoint, and the piano. But all this time he continued to perfect himself on the guitar, to explore all its artistic potentialities. Andrès Segovia, convinced of Bream's immense talent, had meanwhile given him valuable advice, criticism, instruction—and praise.

Bream gave his first concert on the guitar at Cheltenham, England, in 1947, when he was only fourteen. His first recital as a mature artist came four years later, at Wigmore Hall in London, when he became the first British guitarist ever to give a recital. The *Daily Telegraph* in London spoke of him as "an artist of great taste and intelligence as well as technically a master of his instrument." A tour of Great Britain, under the auspices of the Art Council, followed, supplemented by appearances with major concert societies and broadcasts over the radio. To extend the available repertory for the guitar— already enriched through Segovia's efforts—Bream spent a good deal of his time in libraries in England and France in search of old and forgotten music for the guitar, to find suitable pieces from the sixteenth, seventeenth, and eighteenth centuries that could be effectively transcribed from a keyboard instrument for the guitar. In time Bream helped to resurrect many a composer long since in discard whose compositions for guitar made for rewarding listening—old masters such as Luis Milan of the sixteenth century. Bream also adapted for the guitar numerous works by the better-known old masters,

149

among them Frescobaldi, Purcell, Johann Sebastian Bach, and Rameau.

Bream soon divided his programs between the guitar and the lute. This was probably an inevitable development in Bream's concert life since the lute had been a direct ancestor of the guitar, but had been pushed by the latter instrument out of the concert hall and into the museum. The lute, like the guitar, was a plucked instrument, but it had a round body shaped like a half pear. It enjoyed its greatest prominence in the sixteenth century, when it occupied the same significant status as the piano does today. Composers then wrote important compositions for it; the lute was used to accompany singers; it was played in homes; it was a basic element in sixteenth-century orchestras. The heyday of lute music came in England between 1550 and 1620—during the Elizabethan age—when the country's foremost instrumental composers produced a repertory well in excess of two thousand compositions.

The most significant of these composers was John Dowland (1562–1626), probably the greatest lute performer of his generation. Dowland is still remembered and still admired, but other lute composers, long since forgotten, were also productive. These included such masters as Vincenzo Galilei in the sixteenth century, the father of the world-famous astronomer; and Sylvius Leopold Weiss, in the seventeenth. Feeling strongly that the lute creation of these and other old masters had still sufficient musical interest to fascinate discriminating present-day music lovers, Julian Bream soon decided to perfect himself on that old instrument and frequently to divide his program between that instrument and the guitar. It is through his efforts that the lute, after so many years of neglect, has become familiar to the present generation of music audiences.

Bream's success began fanning out slowly as he toured Great Britain and was frequently heard over the radio. Then came a temporary interruption in his career (though not in the making of music) when he had to spend three years in military service as was demanded by the National Service in England. In uniform, he was permitted to pursue his musical interests by playing in the Royal Artillery Band; during this period he was also able to study the cello.

With his service in uniform completed, Bream's concert life could be resumed. Important television appearances, performances at world-famous festivals in Germany, Holland, and Italy, and recordings—all these helped to spread his fame and talent the world over. In 1958 he made his first tour of the United States, his debut taking place in New York City in a concert in which he played both the guitar and the lute. "Some of the most exquisite instrumental sounds that might be expected to fill a New York concert hall this season were produced by Julian Bream in his New York debut," reported a critic for *Musical America*. After one of his concerts, in Washington, D.C., Paul Hume, noted critic of the *Post*, said: "Bream's playing was a thing of polished style, constantly gleaming in the changing lights and shadows he casts by his sensitive touch and understanding phrasing. His guitar playing is something quite magnificent, the still more unusual and glowing vitality of his handling of the lute holds us spellbound."

Young, handsome, dark-haired, Bream makes an immediate favorable impression as he steps briskly across the stage. The effect grows on the audience when he starts playing. Every part of his body seems to be involved in the making of music. His highly expressive face reflects even the subtlest change of emotion in the music.

Young Americans are particularly fascinated by his music making, and some of Bream's greatest successes in this country have come on college campuses. At the University of Connecticut, in the very middle of a concert, the audience had to be transported into a larger auditorium seating three thousand, because so many students were noisily demanding admission into the smaller, overcrowded hall. At Vassar there was also such a huge overflow that the students had to be crowded into the aisles, and some even packed Bream's dressing room. At Harvard his concert was sold out almost as soon as it had been announced. Thus Julian Bream has served as a catalyzing agent between the distant past and the vital and vibrant tomorrow.

INDEX

Aldeburgh Festival, England, 121
Algemeen Handelsblad, quoted,
    134–135
Allen, Steve, show, 13, 17
Amsterdam, 46
Amsterdam Concertgebouw Or-
    chestra, 46, 134
Ashkenasi, Shmuel, 130–132
Aspen (Colorado) Music Festival,
    135
Athens, Greece, 79
Auer, Leopold, 39, 57
Aurora, Colorado, 138
Australia, 79, 128

Bachaus, William, 37
Baku, Azerbaijan, 122
Baltimore, Maryland, 35
Baltimore Symphony, 135
Barbirolli, Sir John, quoted, 129
Barenboim, Daniel, 125–129
Bar-Ilian, David, 133–136
Bar-Ilian, Wilmetta, 135–136
Bartlett and Robertson, 138
Baudouin, King, 35
Belgium, 29
    (See also Brussels)
Ben-Haim, Paul, 125
Berlin, 35, 84, 93, 101, 107, 113
Berlin Die Welt, quoted, 132
Berlin Kurier, quoted, 134

Berlin Morganpost, quoted, 39
Berlin Philharmonic, 54, 134–135
Berlioz, Hector, 147
Bernstein, Leonard, 39, 41, 145
Biancolli, Louis, quoted, 17, 61, 64,
    71, 76
Black, Frank, 45
Blinder, Naoum, 59–61
Boehm, Karl, 134–135
Bolivia, 86–90
Boston, 113
Boston Globe, 93
Boston Herald, 33
Boston Symphony, 38–39, 46
Boulanger, Nadia, 128
Bream, Julian, 147–152
Britten, Benjamin, 121
Brooklyn, 77
Brussels, Belgium, 29, 46, 71, 90,
    100, 112, 132
Budapest, 117
Buenos Aires, 126–127
Buffalo Philharmonic, 41
Busch, Adolf, 78

Cahn, Sammy, 24
Canada, 53, 55
    (See also names of cities, as
    Toronto)
Cape Town Times, quoted, 39

INDEX

Capet, Lucien, 92
Carnegie Hall, 14, 19, 23, 26, 32, 46, 61, 66, 83–85, 98, 113–114, 124, 135
Casadesus, Robert, 30
Casals, Pablo, 75–76, 124
  quoted, 75
Chasins, Abram, 16
  quoted, 17, 25
Cheltenham, England, 149
Chicago, 104, 144
Chicago Orchestra, 39, 104
Chopin, Frédéric, 137
Chotzinoff, Samuel, 45, 83
Christian Science Monitor,
  quoted, 39
Cincinnati Orchestra, 135
Cleveland, 89
Cleveland Orchestra, 35, 41, 50, 69–70, 73, 89, 94
Cliburn, Van, 13–28, 46
Cochabamba, Bolivia, 88
Colette, quoted, 91
Como, Lake, Italy, 32
Culture and Life, 49

Dallas, Texas, 45
Dallas Morning News, 61
Darasch, Arthur, quoted, 54
Davidoff, Karl, 122
Delson, V., quoted, 104–105
Denver Symphony, 139
De Pachmann, Vladimir, 51
Dorlick, Nina, 107
Dowland, John, 150
Downes, Olin, 30
  quoted, 31, 46, 83–84
Durgin, Cyrus, quoted, 93–94

Edinburgh Festival, 65, 73, 79, 94
Einstein, Albert, 84
Eisenhower, President, 15, 23, 35, 58, 97
Elie, Rudolph, quoted, 33
Elizabeth, Queen Mother, of Belgium, 29, 87, 100, 112, 132
Elman, Mischa, 87–88
England, 133, 148–149, 151
Ericsom, Raymond, quoted, 26
Europe, 35, 39, 42, 46, 54–55, 65, 71, 78, 84, 90, 128, 132, 148
  (See also names of countries, as Germany)

Far East, 79, 94
Feher, Ilona, 131
Fiedler, Arthur, 89
Fischer, Edwin, 127
Fizdale, Robert, 138, 142–145
Flamini, Carlo, 88
Fleisher, Leon, 29–36
Fleisher, Raymond, 31
Florence, Italy, 101, 113, 123
Florida, 72
Fonda, Jean, 95
Founier, Pierre, 91–96
Francescatti, Zino, 88
  quoted, 87–88
Frankel, Max, quoted, 22
Frankenstein, Alfred, quoted, 49, 77
Fürtwangler, Wilhelm, quoted, 127

Galamian, Ivan, 89
Galilei, Vincenzo, 150
Gallon, Jean, 92
Garfield, John, 62

154

Geltser, Ekaterina, 112
Geneva, Switzerland, 15, 86, 95, 97
Germany, 93, 113, 134
  (See also Berlin)
Gide, André, quoted, 91
Gilels, Emil, 21, 29, 97–102, 123,
  134–135
Gingold, Josef, 89
Glazunov, 112
Glière, 121
Gold, Arthur, 138, 142–145
Gorodnitsky, Sascha, 77
Gould, Glenn, 49–56
Graffman, Gary, 37–43
Graffman, Naomi, 42
Graffman, Vladimir, 39
Granada, Spain, 148
Grassi, Antonio de, 89
Great Neck, Long Island, 73
Greece, 79–80
Green Bay, Wisconsin, 141
Grossman, Walter, 72
Guerrero, Albert, 53

Haaretz, quoted, 55
Hadley, Henry, 83
Haifa, 133
Harrison, Jay S., quoted, 121, 124
Hauptmann, Gerhart, 84
Heifetz, Jascha, 64, 111
Hekking, André, 92
Hendl, Walter, 39
Horowitz, Vladimir, 25, 37–38,
  43–46, 99
Horszowski, Mieczyslaw, 78
Houser, Frank, 89
Houston, Texas, 19
Hume, Paul, quoted, 54, 89, 151
Hurok, Sol, 62, 128, 132

Iceland, 78–79
Indianapolis Symphony, 40
Israel, 55, 64, 66, 71, 79, 125–128,
  131–133
Israel Philharmonic, 133, 136
Istomin, Eugene, 62, 73, 75–80
Italy, 41, 128
  (See also names of cities, as
  Rome)

Jackson, Mississippi, 43
Janis, Byron, 37–38, 43–47
Japan, 94, 113
Jerusalem, 65
Johnson, Harriet, quoted, 33–34,
  94
Judson, Arthur, 17, 19, 89

Kastner, Santiago, quoted, 148
Kaye, Nora, 66
Kennedy, President, 71
Kennedy, Mrs. John F., 71, 87
Kharkov, 112
Khatchaturian, Abram, 120
  quoted, 25
Khrushchev, Premier, 15, 22, 58,
  97
Kiev, 58, 105, 112
Kilgore, Texas, 16, 18, 22
Klein, Howard, quoted, 42
Klemperer, Otto, 38
Klin, Russia, 27
Kogan, Leonid, 102, 122
Kol Israel Orchestra, 131, 136
Kolodin, Irving, quoted, 46, 53, 72
Kondrashin, Kiril P., 23
  quoted, 47
Koussevitzky, Sviatoslav, 115
Kozolupoff, Semeon, 122

Kriminiesz, Russia, 59
Krips, Josef, 39

Lackey, Mary Elizabeth, 82–83
Lang, Paul Henry, quoted, 72, 121–122
Laredo, Jaime, 86–90
Leningrad, 55, 58, 112, 115
Lhevinne, Josef, 45
Lhevinne, Rosina, 19–20
Lindeblit, Vera, 66–67
Liszt, Franz, 137
Little Orchestra Society, 42
Little Symphony Society, 78
Liverpool Philharmonic, 38
London, 42, 84–86, 113, 124, 129, 133, 147–149
London *Daily Telegraph*, quoted, 39, 149
London Philharmonic, 38, 42, 93, 127
London *Times*, quoted, 128, 145
Lowe, Jack, 138–142
Luboschutz and Nemenoff, 138
Lucerne, 94
Lyons, James, quoted, 86

McKeesport, Pennsylvania, 44
Macmillan, Ernest, 54
Maier, Guy, 138
Mainardi, Enrico, 127
Manhattan Symphony, 83
Marcus, Adele, 45
Markevitch, Igor, 127
Mazurkevich, Yuri, quoted, 116
Meckler, Ruth, 90
Mendelssohn, Felix and Fanny, 137
Menton, France, 79
Menuhin, Yehudi, 82

Miaskovsky, 120
Mikoyan, First Deputy Premier, 22
Miller, Frank, 72
Minneapolis Symphony, 39
Mitchell, Howard, 132
Mitropoulos, Dimitri, 17, 137
    quoted, 70
Monteux, Pierre, 32, 59
Morris, Mrs. Harold, 39
Moscow, 14, 16, 18–20, 29, 55, 58, 100–102, 106–107, 112, 115–117, 120–123, 132
Moscow State Symphony, 47
Munch, Charles, 39
Musical America, 44, 86, 143
    quoted, 115, 151

Naples, 128
National Symphony, 132
NBC Symphony Orchestra, 45, 72–73
Near East, 127–128
Neuhaus, Heinrich, 100, 106
    quoted, 49
New York City, 14, 19, 26–27, 32, 34, 39–40, 42, 46, 59–60, 66, 71–73, 77, 83, 86, 93, 98, 104, 113–114, 124, 128, 133, 135, 143–144, 151
New York *Herald Tribune*, 61, 72, 94, 121, 124, 144
    quoted, 46, 60, 128
New York Philharmonic, 17, 32, 39, 41, 65, 69–70, 78, 133–134, 145
New York *Post*, 33, 94
    quoted, 128
New York *Sun*, 46

New York Times, The, 22–23, 26, 30, 46, 70, 76, 87, 98–99, 103, 114, 121, 123, 128
quoted, 35, 40, 47, 50, 141
New York Times Magazine, 62
New York *World,* 83
New York *World Telegram,* 17, 71
New York *World Telegram and Sun,* 61, 76
quoted, 98, 135
New Zealand, 128

Oborin, Lev, 115
Odessa, 99–100, 105–106, 111–112
Odessa Symphony, 112
Oistrakh, David, 29, 100, 111–117
Oistrakh, Igor, 116
Ormondy, Eugene, 41, 78–79, 98

Paganini, Niccolo, 147
Paris, 42, 50, 91–94, 124, 128, 144, 147
Paris Conservatory Orchestra, 46
Parmenter, Ross, quoted, 23
Pattison, Lee, 138
Perpignan, France, 76, 79
Persinger, Louis, 59, 82
Philadelphia, 40–41, 78, 89, 98, 131–132
Philadelphia *Enquirer,* quoted, 98
Philadelphia Orchestra, 41, 78–79, 98
Philadelphia Symphonette, 40
Philharmonic Hall, Lincoln Center, 38, 66, 145
Pittsburgh, 45
Pittsburgh Symphony, 45
Poulenc, Francis, quoted, 145

Prades, France, 75–76, 78–79
Prague, 101, 107, 123
Pravda, quoted, 55
Prokofiev, Serge, 97, 120
Puerto Rico, 76, 79, 140

Rachmaninoff, Serge, 27, 40
Ricci, Ruggiero, 81–86
Richter, Sviatoslav, 103–109, 120–122
quoted, 25
Riegger, Wallingford, 42
Ringold, Bertha, 99
Rochester, New York, 139
Rodriguez, Valma, 86
Rodzinski, Artur, 78
Rome, 113, 128
Rose, Leonard, 62, 69–75
Rose, Minna, 73–74
Rosenfeld, John, quoted, 61
Rosenthal, Rikki, 35
Rostropovich, Mstislav, 119–124
Rubinstein, Artur, 25, 30, 99
quoted, 31, 99–100
Russia, 14–15, 22–24, 27, 29, 46–47, 54, 57–59, 65, 77, 94, 97, 100–101, 103, 111–112, 115, 132
(*See also* names of cities, as Odessa)

Sacramento, California, 89
St. Joseph, Missouri, 141
Salmanov, Vadim, 55
Salmond, Felix, 72
Salzburg, 35, 94, 127
San Francisco, 31, 59, 82–83, 88–89
San Francisco *Chronicle,* 77

San Francisco Symphony, 32, 39, 59, 89
San Juan, Puerto Rico, 76, 79, 140
Saturday Review, 53, 72
Scandinavia, 101, 113
Schnabel, Artur, 31–33, 36–37
Schonberg, Harold C., quoted, 38, 62–63, 65–66, 99, 114
Schuman, William, 19, 145
Seattle, Washington, 34, 71, 79
Segovia, Andrès, 147–149
Serkin, Rudolf, 78
Seroff, Victor I., 102
    quoted, 101
Sevitsky, Fabian, 40
Shorr, Lev, 31
Shostakovich, Dimitri, 114, 120
Shreveport, Louisiana, 18
Siena, 128
Siloti, Alexander, 77
Siloti, Kariena, 77
Smith, Leo, 53
Solfeggio, 88
Sor, Fernando, 147
South Africa, 78, 94
South America, 42, 46, 65, 71, 78, 94, 128, 148
Soviet Music, 104
Soviet Union (*see* Russia)
Spain, 147–148
Stern, Isaac, 57–68, 73, 75
Sternberg, William, 41
Stokowski, Leopold, 128
Stoliarsky, Pytor, 111–112, 116
Stratford, Ontario, 55
Stuckenschmidt, H. H., quoted, 54
Svedoff, Constantin, 77
Symphony of the Air, 128

Szell, George, 17, 35, 41, 51, 94
    quoted, 70, 88

Tanglewood, 79, 135
Taubman, Howard, quoted, 70–71, 76, 87, 98, 103–104, 114–115, 121, 123–124, 128
Teheran, 80
Tel Aviv, 64–65, 125, 131
Thomson, Virgil, quoted, 61, 94, 144
Time magazine, 51–52, 129
Tkach, Jacob, 99
"Tonight" show, 13, 17
Toronto, Canada, 53–54, 144
Toronto Symphony, 54
Toscanini, Arturo, 72–73, 133
Town Hall, New York City, 40, 93, 140, 144
Tucson, Arizona, 26
Turkey, 113

Ukraine, the, 105, 112
United States, 14–16, 18, 22–23, 27, 46, 54, 84, 88, 90, 97–98, 100, 103–104, 107, 111, 113, 124, 132–133, 135, 148
    (*See also* names of cities, as Chicago)

Van Heusen, James, 24
Vengerova, Mme. Isabella, 40
Vermillion, South Dakota, 138
Vienna, 50, 84, 127
Vishnevskaya, Galina, 124
Von Karajan, Herbert, 54
Von Papen, Chancellor, 84
Voroshilov, Marshal, 22
Vronsky and Babin, 138

Walker, James J., 83
Walter, Bruno, 73
Warsaw, 112, 117
Washington, D.C., 34, 54, 72, 89, 132
Washington *Post*, 89, 151
Weiss, Sylvius Leopold, 150
Whittemore, Arthur, 138–142
Wolfe, Ralph, 77

Wolpe, Stefan, 42
World War II, 84–85, 93, 100, 113, 116, 122, 134, 140
Wright, June Dickson, 47

Ysaÿe, Eugène, 29, 62

Zakin, Alexander, 61
Zimbalist, Efrem, 131

ABOUT THE AUTHOR

David Ewen has written over forty books on every facet of music—serious and popular—for adults and for young people. *Time* Magazine described him as "music's interpreter to the American people," and his books have been translated into over a dozen foreign languages.

Mr. Ewen published his first book in 1931, and since then not a year has passed without at least one of his titles appearing on a publisher's list. In the field of serious music his most popular works include *Encyclopedia of the Opera, Encyclopedia of Concert Music, The Complete Book of 20th Century Music, The World of Great Composers, David Ewen Introduces Modern Music,* and *The New Book of Modern Composers.* He has written biographies of George Gershwin, Jerome Kern, and Richard Rodgers. Among his books on popular music are *The Complete Book of the American Musical Theater, Panorama of American Popular Music,* and *The Life and Death of Tin Pan Alley.*

In 1962–1963, Mr. Ewen wrote and co-produced a series of fifty-two broadcasts tracing the history of American popular music, which was beamed all over the world, in two dozen languages and dialects, by the Voice of America. Mr. Ewen's books for young people include biographies of George Gershwin, Jerome Kern, Richard Rodgers, Leonard Bernstein, Arturo Toscanini, Johann Strauss, Joseph Haydn, Irving Berlin, and Cole Porter.